EVERY STORY IS A MIRACLE

UPDATED AND CORRECTED VERSION OF
THIS IS ME

GARY D. WILSON
AND <u>NOT</u> HIS COMPUTER

Author's Tranquility Press
MARIETTA, GEORGIA

Copyright © 2022 by Gary D. Wilson

All rights reserved. No part of this publication may be reproduced, distributed or transmitted in any form or by any means, including photocopying, recording, or other electronic or mechanical methods, without the prior written permission of the publisher, except in the case of brief quotations embodied in critical reviews and certain other noncommercial uses permitted by copyright law. For permission requests, write to the publisher, addressed "Attention: Permissions Coordinator," at the address below.

Gary D. Wilson/Author's Tranquility Press
2706 Station Club Drive SW
Marietta, GA/30060
www.authorstranquilitypress.com

This is a work of non-fiction.

Everyday Is A Miracle/Gary D. Wilson
Paperback: 978-1-958554-26-5
eBook: 978-1-958554-27-2

TABLE OF CONTENTS

THIS IS ME 1
CHAPTER 1 5
CHAPTER 2 9
CHAPTER 3 17
CHAPTER 4 28
CHAPTER 5 38
CHAPTER 6 46
CHAPTER 7 54
CHAPTER 8 61
CHAPTER 9 69
CHAPTER 10 97
CHAPTER 11 119
AND A NEW ME HAS BEGUN 121
CHAPTER 12 122
CHAPTER 13 126
CHAPTER 14 146
CHAPTER 15 154

DEDICATION

First off...I would like to thank my mom for being behind me 110%!

Although the book might not show her very well, she has taken many 3-hour drives to see me in the hospital. I love my mom and always will!

Plus, I would also like to thank my boys and my daughter-in-law for being behind me while I wrote this book.

Mostly, the folks that want to see some things about me and the circumstances that we can learn about life.

WE ARE NOT ALONE GOING THROUGH THESE TOUGH TIMES!!

THIS IS ME

There are so many things that happen to all of us. The thing is though, that it's not things that happen to us that makes us. It is what we do ABOUT it that makes us who we are.

When you go to a store and buy something, a piece of candy for two dollars and twenty-four cents. You go outside, count your change and you find that you were not given the correct change back. The whole thing could then start a total episode. Based on what you do as well as what the clerk does.

You could just say, "Oh well" and not worry about it or you could go nuts and yell at the cashier. Or, something, anything, in between. But then the cashier has the same options.

The cashier can apologize and give the correct change, or they can just deny any, "You are wrong" and decline any action. You two can both stand there and yell back and forth at each other. Or you two can both be courteous with each other and come to a mutually satisfying closing.

Those are the things that make this little THING called "LIFE" go round.

We all have decisions to make. From the minute the alarm goes off in the morning, picking out your clothes, deciding what you want for dinner and up until you go to bed each night. Just remember, we ALL have decisions to make. These decisions we all make, we make OURSELVES. We are each then responsible for ourselves as well as how we do things to others. It is 1996. I lived in a small town in Connecticut. Ansonia. A nice small town I am happily married and have two GREAT boys. Craig and Todd. They are 7 and 3 years old Now, I am not being too one-sided, but I KNOW that they are the two best kids in the world.

Your kids are running a close 3! Hey, that's fine by me!

My wife and I are having some problems. By now, we are married since 1986. We are having some problems. I am a "workaholic".

I am working for XEROX in New York City. I enjoy my job. I have started as a technician, fixing customers machines in their offices in Fairfield County, Connecticut. But I decided that I do not feel like turning screw drivers for the rest of my life. Along with this job, I also work a part-time job at SAM'S CLUB in Orange CT.

So, I have to make a decision to make a big change. I have just gotten a new job with the same company in New York City. No, not fixing machines. Instead, working in their offices working with the truck company in New Jersey handling the delivering, moving and pick-ups of Xerox machines within Manhattan and New York City. New York City is the second busiest area in the country. I assist in handling about five to fifteen million dollars per month! WOW! I really like my job. No, it is not so fantastic, but it certainly is not hum drum either.

My commute into work each day is two to two and a half hours…each way!

I am also an EMS volunteer for my town, Ansonia, Connecticut. The town has its own Rescue and Medical Service run by volunteers. We handle everything from motor vehicle accidents and vehicle extrication with the Jaws-Of-Life to sick calls and heart attacks. I wear a portable pager with me almost all time for "just in case". I am honored one month to be chosen Volunteer of the Month with the second-highest volunteer responders! I am kept quite busy all hours and all times, midnights, evenings, days. Weekends, Holidays and days off. I know I am doing this quite a bit, But I also know that volunteering for EMS is important. I know I feel it as a commitment.

Again, my wife and I are having some problems. She is VERY much behind me as well as the organization. She knows and understands what I am doing with EMS. Many times, like when there is a party going on at my house, for a family birthday for a niece or someone. I ask her if she minded that I take the call. She usually says OK. Whether from my house, the grocery store, or any place in between or getting up in the middle of the night.

EMS is not something I can just give up and go away from. It is a sign of, well, as I said before, it is a commitment. To the citizens and neighbors of my town. Knowing that if or when something happens, someone will be there to help them. Instead, I have decided to just leave my New York City job.

My wife and I know that I cannot just up and leave my job, so we have to just be patient and careful and look for a new place. I am looking around and I see one possibility. A sales job not far from my house. Selling Xerox machines. I can stay closer to home and try to work in the US.

So now I have found a much closer place. Granted, I am not so great at sales, but my number one priority, my family, comes first. With the way things are going, there is a definite possibility that things terribly awful can happen here! Something that neither one wants. I can really get the US part back! The problem is, though, that the workaholic part of me won't go away. I also do some part-time work whenever I get the chance. You see, my wife and I have decided a long time ago that, yes, we do believe that nannies are good and all. But we had decided that either one of would stay home with the boys and one would work. So that is what we are doing.

A lot has happened since then, but first, let me get you to know a bit more about me and where and how I have come about:

CHAPTER 1

It is January 9, 1964. My mom goes into the hospital. She is pregnant. She has two boys already. One is one year old, the other is two. Hmmmm, there is no guy there. Just mom. Seems that she and her husband were having some very serious situations. It is best this way. I have, I guess literally, never laid eyes on him.

I guess it is mom and her two boys. So now it is she and her family and two boys. One is one year old and the other is two.

Mom goes into the hospital; she has two boys at home. Now she has two more boys. **WOW!** Four boys! But there are complications. Mom should not be having these two new boys for two and a half months! So, she has the twins but because we are "premies". Turns out that we are born two and a half months premature. I guess we could not wait to just get up and out and see the world! There are complications and the doctors are not sure if we would survive the night.

Due to us being born too early, mom wants to have us boys baptized. But because of the unexpected early time, mom has us blessed as "Baby *Pf'* and "Baby B". The baptism goes well and all is done. We are all in the hospital for as long as is determined necessary and then, well, off to home now!

I have my "big brother", that is, my seven minute earlier twin brother, that, even to this day he ALWAYS reminds me and my two older brothers now.

They say that LIFE is what happens when you are busy making plans. I guess that I can say that I cannot disagree with that at all! Well, again, I guess this thing called LIFE happens.

My next to oldest brother for whatever reason, has to have some kind of plate put in his head. You know, even to this day I am not sure why. I mean, I know there is a valid reason, I know he knows why, as well as anyone else. I just don't know. I know they are not trying to hide anything, but, OH WELL! I know he knows about it and all the info, because I know he tried to get into the Army and he did not mention it. But when they did find out about it, he is discharged.

Well, anyway, getting back to the past....

Mom is now back home with her four guys. Without her husband. But she does have her family with her. Giving her whatever help and support they can.

So, she has us and she is doing whatever she can. But things are getting tough for her. She speaks with her family. Her sister agrees to help her by adopting two of the boys and she would keep two. She figures that at least they will all stay within the family.

She consults the state. Well, unfortunately, they decline. So, she is now back to square one. She, as far as I am concerned, she shows that she loves ALL of us.

Well, things go and take one step down. I am not sure just how old my twin and I are, but we are big enough to be walking around now. I guess we are around four or so. We somehow get a hold of a cigarette lighter. I am not sure where mom is. Maybe in just another room. Maybe at work. Are we at my mom's house? My aunt's place? Not sure.

Well, again, my twin and I get a hold of a cigarette lighter. We are doing whatever with it. My next to oldest brother is in the area. Somehow, he is in the middle of us, and, well, let's just say that things go down and somehow, he gets turned up in fire. No, he is not dead or anything like that. However, his stomach is burnt. He eventually has some skin grafts done. The grafts are pulled eventually from the legs to help cover whatever body burns. Well, I will say that he seems to be one heck of a fighter!!

Eventually, mom goes to the state and at least my twin and I are put in an orphanage. Maybe my brothers too. I think it is all four of us, but not quite definite. But I think so.

I know it may sound weird to some, but I can actually, somehow, remember the orphanage. I can remember a white crib and blue walls. People seem to talk a lot about how bad and gross that the orphanages are. How bad the kids are treated. Well, I do not think that mom would have put us in such an awful place. It seems like she has doing whatever she can to keep us together.

Anyway, we are there now, I think all four of us. The situation, briefly, is this: Mom has split from her husband.

Four boys. One is in good shape. One has a plate put in his head plus burn damage to his stomach and neck. One set of twins. Both born two and a half months pre-mature. Mom tries to have to keep all of us together between her sister and her. I am not sure if my aunt is married. I assume so.

All four of us are now placed in an orphanage. Mom does not want to do this, but at least they are being cared for. Not being shortened on food, bed or anything bad. She is hoping for just a little while. But things change. Again.

We have spent about six months here now. The state, orphanage and mom have come to an agreement. We will all be put in a foster home. Together. My mom's only request/requirement is that we all keep the same religion, Protestant. At least then we will each have SOMETHING in common. All parties agree. So, off we go to a Foster home.

Chapter 2

Well, off we all go on to this next step. This thing called "LIFE". All four of us go into the Foster system. Again, something that many people give bad raps to.

We go into this woman's house. A nice size house. Nice size yard. Nice neighborhood.

A single woman. Hmmm... One older brother and three sisters. So well, not quite like an orphanage, but some nice people. They each seem to be smiling and laughing a lot.

We get our rooms and all. I am rooming with my twin. Two beds and a closet and two dressers. It is a nice size rooms. A couple of windows too.

The windows turn out to be some of my favorite areas. They are great when it is raining. I get to see the rainfall and all. Plus, I get to see the lightning and hear the thunder. Granted, sometimes the lightning and thunderstorms scare the heck out of some kids, but I love it! It seems that with all the chaos in the sky with the lightning and thunder going on sometimes, I feel like this is my own world!

All is calm and, well, everything seems to be just nice and fine here. This seems to be a place that I feel very nice and very comfortable. Eventually, my twin and I finally start this thing called school. The kids and teachers seem to be pretty neat. But I am having a problem with my temper. For almost no reason at all, I am having temper tantrums. I do remember Miss Jordan. My first-grade teacher. For some reason I am having one of my tantrums. I remember her coming out to the hallway with me, after I take my shoes off and throwing them. I remember her coming out to the hallway, sitting on the floor with me and giving me a big hold and hug. Right there. On the floor. I do remember, and being happy, that this is the last tantrum I have had in school. I am not sure if it is the last in my life, but I do know it is the last in school.

I do remember, also, trying to fool the teachers with my twin in school. I remember in the second grade, we were both wearing the same clothes. We decided to play a prank and switch class's right from the start of the day.

I went into his class and him into mine. I am a bit scared, granted. But we decided to try it. I am not sure what happened with Miss. Jordan and my twin, but his teacher knew me right off the bat! Class had just about started, and his teacher told me to go out and get my brother and swap back! No hesitation. She just told me right out and out to go back to my class and to send my brother back into his correct class.

Eventually I am going to the park with my brothers. One thing I eventually realize that mom does not drive. We have no car. We walk everywhere. Even to the grocery store. I am begging for mom to treat me like a big boy. So, she finally lets me carry this big five-pound bag of potatoes. Seems like a nice size. Not real big, but hey, I can handle it! I'm a big boy!

It's a long walk, but hey, we can all handle it! Walking is good for everyone. So thankfully we get home and I can't wait to put this bag down! Again, my mom does not drive, but my big brother and big sister from my NEW family does!

My new family has one big brother and three big sisters, but they do not all live there though. Two of my sisters are married, as is one brother. One sister is single...for now.

So now there are the four of us plus one sister in the house, but one other brother and two more sisters out of the house. Seems kind of strange, but yet, we are still like one big family. The holidays especially. When everyone comes to the house with their husbands and wives and kids! Is like one large party!

There is one small thing that my twin and I are going through though. Seems that my actual birthday is unknown. Or at least not quite definite. So we go through some dates, and then finally confirm 9 January 1964 is the date. Again, nothing too big because whenever it is any kid's birthday party, we ALWAYS have a big party. I mean balloons, cake and hats, I do wonder sometimes where dad is. I mean there are four other kids here. So where is their dad?

I finally find out that their dad was in a bad car accident. Now, I do not have the particulars, I have just heard that he was in a real bad car accident and was in a home or something like that. He could not stay at home, Again, I do not know any specifics, just this bit.

Their whole family seems OK with everything.

Sometimes, there are more kids here. My new mom believes in helping kids whenever she can. It seems like she has a whole lot of love to give!

There is one guy in a wheelchair that has come to stay at the house I think twice, Jessie. Then there also is a young guy that is young enough to need a high chair. Then there is Joe. I don't know a lot about him, about the only thing that I do know is that he was in the Navy.

Then there is Bill and Jimmy. I know that they have been here for a while. Not as long as my brothers and I, but still.

I call my new mom, "Mom" because is just what she seems to be to me. A mom. My new mom makes sure we go to church. Is sort of strange in a way. Because she goes to one church and by three brothers and I go to a different one. That's right; my birth mom wanted all four of us to stay the same religion. My new mom is Catholic and I am Protestant, like my brothers. My new mom and the whole and big family, eight or more go to the Catholic Church together on holidays, but every other Sunday we go to my other church with my three brothers. My mom is VERY religious. She seems to live the right way. She is not one of those folks that say one thing and does another. She seen to live the "right" way and teaches us also. As well as any and all kids here.

Well, anyway, the foster home seems to actually be going very well! You know, on the news I am hearing and seeing so many bad things about foster homes or foster parents. The thing is thou, that it is all bad things that I am hearing. To be totally honest, yes, there may be some bad foster folks. But they can only be the bottom two percent. My foster mom and foster family teach and show us so much love! That is, love and work.

Mom and all of her kids are showing us this thing called love, but not just by hugging and squeezing and kissing us. They are showing it by showing us about responsibility. Whether it is by having us make our beds in the morning, changing our clothes or being home in time for dinner. But mostly about being honest and sincere. Yes, we are all young enough to play, but chores come into life too.

Mom is showing us so much of this love. Whether she is cook dinner, helping us with our homework or disciplining us when we are bad, we know that she and her whole family, love us.

My brothers and I spend a lot of time going to the park together. AAHHH the Park! A lot of things happen there. My brothers and I go down there quite a bit. Sometimes to play games, sometimes to go and act, sometimes for 4TH of July parties. We all do enjoy going there. I do some acting. I cannot wait for this Easter Play coming up! I am so excited and happy about it. I get to sing! Solo! There was a try out a few weeks ago. About a thousand kids tried out for the part. My next to oldest brother, remember the one that was burnt, tried for this song, "Easter Parade". He always said that he has such a great voice. HAH! I got the part!! I am so excited and so scared!

Well, during practice one day, the director pulls me aside. Seems that there is a new kid that has just come into the play and acting group. Well, it seems that he has a real good voice. So, the managers decide to give him the solo. I am so upset. But, well, life does go on. I still have a part in one of the plays.

I am Cratchet, from A "Christmas Carol". But, well, not to brag, I am the best Cratchet there ever was!

Well, again, the park is a great place. The 4th of July parties as well as the summer time weekends are great! Between the friends there, Kenny M, Johnny L, and Jennifer. We are all good friends from the summer parties plus with them living so close to me. Johnny's dad is a fireman at the firehouse. We all can't wait. They are building a new firehouse down the street from me now. Johnny's dad, a fireman, will be working out of the new place. Plus, it is right down the street from me from home.

I know it seems strange in a way that I work at my age, eleven or twelve. But this Office Store, selling typewriters and office stuff, is two houses down the street from home. Plus, well, I guess it helps. Not with money or anything like that, but hey, I guess I am learning about this stuff called responsibility. Going to "work". Being responsible in doing whatever my job is, etc. I guess you can say that I am learning, in a way, to be a man. My job is just basically to keep things in order. Wipe the dust off some things. Nothing big, obviously. Just stuff.

My brothers and I have been at the foster home for quite a while now. Eight years now. I guess it is about that time again. It is now down to just the four of us. Seems that mom's four kids are all grown up and married now. No, they have not disappeared. They are all around. Not in the same house. But for holidays, weddings, summer picnics in the huge back yard, grocery shopping. We are all together. But now it is time to move on.

My oldest brother leaves. He has all of his clothes packed up. We just basically say good bye. Hug and kiss and all. Then, well, he goes away. Then it is my next brother's turn. Again, no parties or anything like that. Just our hugs and kisses and all.

Well, at night though, my twin and I do cry at night. We do miss them. I get up this one night to go to the bathroom, I hear mom. Crying. She misses them too. I know she does. She is just being strong for the two of us. I hear her saying prayers. Asking prayers and blessings for them.

Now it is my twin's time and I. Seems that we are going together. Seems a bit different though. My brothers went to two other foster homes. My twin and I are going to an adoptive home. Seems that there is someone out there that either, is willing or wants to, adopt twins! **WOW!** A couple that is actually willing to take on two of ME! I am not sure this is a good thing, I am joking to myself. So, twin and I go off with a case worker to meet these two.

We meet at an IHOP, International House of Pancakes, for a late breakfast. We meet and talk and spend some time there. I ask them what I refer to them as: what do I call them. He answers, "Whatever you do, please don't call me Mr. Wilson. I will keep on looking around looking for Dennis!"

After breakfast the caseworker and my twin and I leave. We get in the car, and she asks what we think. Well, I tell her that they do seem like some nice folks.

Now, I am not so sure that there is anybody in this that would be willing to take ME in. Let alone my twin and I. Please understand that I do not feel down on myself. I just know and understand about taking two kids in. I do not think that there would ever be another chance like this again.

So, my twin and I agree that we should go with this couple. At least we will be together. Granted, without our big brothers, but at least we will not be alone. So, well, away we go!!

Chapter 3

My twin and I are now in a new house. Granted, not as big as our other house, but is nice. Well, one big thing is that we are not far from the firehouse! It is on our same street. The school is a bit further away, but hey! A good walk to and from school is not really a bad thing! I am in good shape. Although I am not really interested in sports like football or baseball, I get along with the walks and all really well.

There is something, uummm, a bit different going on here at this house. My last mom had us going to church every Sunday and all. We were also taught about the United States of America and the British and everything like that. About how proud we should be about being American, The Fourth of July picnics and everything. But things are different now. Here it is, just past July 4th, 1976. Two hundred years of freedom. My old town that I lived in had just built a new walkway around a park so that we could all see the ships going through the river by the George Washington Bridge. They looked so fantastic. To see all of the ships and all of the sails. The re-make all of the big ships!

Now a quick and brief over view of them:

He had spent time in the Navy, along with his brother. In Vietnam, he was also captured and tortured. I am not sure how long he was held, but regardless, it is not something I would want to see or hear anything about being done to anyone. I knew he told me about learning to sleep with one eye open. I am not sure of what he specifically did, but I do know that he was a Navy SEAL and had special training, let alone his "regular" duties.

So far as my newest mom: well, I do not know or remember a lot about what she did. I know she was brought up in this town. The same house. She had gone to the same schools, and we had the same Guidance Counselor. I know she had gone to a Beauty School. But that is where it ends.

Well, it seems my newest mom's religion will not allow her to practice something about dealing with politics. But each Sunday my twin and we with her to her church. Once or twice during the week too. She is hard of hearing using hearing aids, so we sit in a back part of the church, Kingdom Hall, by the handicapped folks. It is actually neat, in a way. I am picking up some sign language and learning some about reading lips. My mom can hear, a little even without the aids, but not well at all.

My dad does not have a religion; He is not sure about this guy called God. So, he does not go to church with us.

My new mom does the hairdressing thing at home. She has ladies come over and she cuts and braids and washes and colors their hair. She seems to do it quite well. She has gone to school for all of this. She has also worked in a salon place too. She is not some "fly-by-might "haircut lady". She is professional beautician that now works out of the house so she can be at home for my twin and I.

My dad, it feels kinda feels strange, calling him a dad. Only because I have never had a dad before.

He is a strong guy. He works for a railroad company, CONRAIL. He has eventually made his way up to General Foreman of the repair and maintenance department. Working all kinds of hours, sometimes overnight, sometimes very long days. There are sometimes, nights especially, when he takes the train into work. Not like the usual commuters though.

You see, the train goes by about two or three blocks from my house. When dad takes the train in, he calls his office and lets them know what he is doing, that he is taking the train in. He leaves the house and goes to the railroad tracks. There is no train stop there, but the driver is radioed ahead and told to expect him. So, the driver slows the train down, my dad runs up to the train, without it stopping, grabs on to the train and leaps onto it! Without it ever stopping! Well, it seems he is in some good shape too! Occasionally I go to work with him. But in a CAR!!!

WOW! It's a big place with trains all over the place! I am going bit nuts seeing all of these things. A kids dream! All these neat trains. And I get to walk and go all around them. He knows all of what he is doing, that's for sure. If any of the guys are having a hard time with any of the trains, he can take care of it. The guys there quickly get to know me, "The boss's kid".

I am watching dad this one time going to a train, taking a two-hundred-pound battery out of the train with one hand, pulling it onto his back and carrying it away on just one arm! WOW! Very impressive!

My dad is a master mechanic. He is "trained in all...and a master of all". He can fix about anything that you give to him. Whether it is a built-up new car or old torn up one, an old locomotive or something made out of wood. He can fix about anything that you place in front of him, regardless. He will look at it, check it out and then fix it. No matter what the problem.

Occasionally, I go to work with him. I get to talk with the guys there. My dad even lets me drive one or two of the trains around. I get to drive the train up on to the big donut thing that transfers the train in to certain tracks for repair work. Yes, my dad is there explaining everything to me. Telling me about the "Dead Man's Pedal". Explaining that the Driver MUST have his foot on there at ALL times. So, if he were to have a heart attack. The train would stop. It also means that he could NOT fall asleep or run out for a cup of coffee.

It is so neat sometimes! Being the General Foreman's son! One night the station needed a boss to handle the whole station. So, they called him in to run the station plus the repair part. Well, talk about being impressed and happy. That for this one time, my dad was in charge of the WHOLE place! Yup, I am the Boss's kid!

Once in a while my brother goes. But not at the same time. I guess one of us at a time is enough.

Life at home was, uummmm, different. Seems that mom is the one who punishes. I am finding out that it is because of him being of maybe hitting us too hard, or losing his temper. Seems that, I guess, that part of Vietnam came home with him. Seems that he has brought some thoughts home with him.

About a year later, it is time for the adoption process to go through. But a tangle in the web, though. Our social worker is not upset, but I guess a bit confused. It seems that she has put in the paperwork for the courts that we are "Identical" twins. Bur my twin has black curly hair and I do not.

You see, my twin does not want us to be twins anymore. Seems that he is, not tired of he and I looking like each other, but I guess just not want to be looking like "someone else". I can agree with that, that's for sure! Everyone skipping on names and all. So, my mom now has to color and perms my hair to look like him! Oh well. So, off we go to get things done. Well, those are not the ONLY changes.

You see, I did not like my name. I had no middle name and, well, I wanted to be named after my father. So now I am a "JR" plus my twin decided to be named different too. He liked his middle name better than his first. He also liked my "new" grandfather's name. So, he changed it too. So now his old middle was his new first and his new middle was different too.

I quickly got a job delivering newspapers. I originally delivered to just one half of my part of town. It was good. I got to get out of the house to deliver newspapers six days a week. Plus, I got to go around my part of tow to collect my customer's weekly money. It was neat. Going around to all of my customer's houses. Sometimes seeing my friends there. Boy was it tough during the rain, though. But when it comes down to it, hey, sometimes it was better off being out in the town delivering newspapers or collecting money, even in the rain, then worrying about being at home sometimes.

Now, please understand, maybe I am making them out as bad parents. Well, they are not. Here the two of them are. Willing to take in two kids, strangers, into their home and raise them. They did teach me things like responsibility and money management.

Eventually my paper route is extended to over twice the size! I now have to handle my whole half of town. It is not easy but well worth it. Granted, I had my dues to pay for living at home and all. But again, RESPONSIBILITY. Things are going OK for me with work and all. I enjoy my paper route so much, along with the bike riding around town, mom and dad even let me buy not only one bike, but two now! I have just bought two ten speed bikes. One is a bit heavier, so I have chosen to use this one for my newspaper route. The other is light weight. Easier for racing and running around town. I love both of my bikes.

Like so many other folks, times are tough. Dad works hard and as much as he can. Mom is a stay-at-home mom. She is also a beautician and does a lot of lady friend's hair. So, for the most part, she stays at home. She does occasionally work for a card parts place, delivering car parts from a supplier's place to different garages. On weekends thou, are real long. Mom, my brother and I deliver newspapers from the back of dad's truck, a Dodge Ram.

On Saturday afternoons a small truck comes to our house. The deliver a lot of Sunday Newspaper parts like the comics, coupon and sports pages. We spend a good few hour putting at least some of the paper together. Then on Sunday, we get up real early, I think it is somewhere around three AM. We are up so early putting the rest done. I think it is somewhere around two to three hundred papers!

My brother, mom and I get in the truck and drive around town delivering papers. My brother and I are in the back of the truck, gate down, sometimes throwing to customers houses. Sometime, just jumping off of the back, running to a front porch, opening up the screen door and putting the paper in. Come rain or shine, this one way of making some cash!

But then again, we do have some of our good times. Like maybe going to the streams. We go out there with all of the trees and bushes and streams. I am asking my mom about maybe going to the water and going for a walk with my shoes on. I know that it may seem like a small thing, but with the water running between my feet and not worrying about any rocks or anything. The water is so clean and clear! Not even thinking about or worried about glass or anything like that. Just enjoying some time outside in the water and in the sun. AAHHH!! Call it natural!

But then again, I feel that sometimes the best time of the day is night time. Just when it comes time to go to bed, I head up there a bit early. I like to read. At any time. I guess that the best time for me is when I am getting ready to hit LALA land. Well, then again, I guess I like reading about any time. It kind of puts me into a different place. I get to put myself right into the book.

My favorite books are "Hardy Boys". I happen to really like the mystery parts. I have about the whole series. About twenty-two or something like that. I like that each book has a different story. There are some of the same players, but others too. It is a matter of, well, exercising my brain. Trying to remember which friend is which, which guy was the bad guy (or gal! hey, equal opportunity!) But I like that I get to step out of my life or my day for a while.

Well, one day it seems my twin does not get home from school. My parents get a call from school. I do not know what is happening here, but eventually I am told that he is no longer coming home. I guess now I have the whole upstairs attic to myself! It is not a big place, but it just a bit bigger.

Well, it seems that my twin is not happy here. We have gone to school, as usual, but for some reason, he is not coming home. We are now about fourteen. I get home and mom and dad are telling me that he is not coming home any more. His choice, not theirs.

It sees that he has sat down with a guidance counselor and has told him some things about us and our parents. About my mom's stick with our names on the fridge.

Yes, I can understand why, but has made his decision. So now my parents are going to court. It seems that he has statements that must be looked at by a judge. We all go into court now. I have been asked about knowing the truth. I am not actually sworn in, but I am asked about what my twin has said. Basically, I denied ALL of what he has said. So now I am heading home now. I have taken over his part of the newspaper deliveries. Now I have double the deliveries about forty-five blocks!

Eventually, for one reason or another, I have another job. I am working at a bakery. Czerkas Bakery in Clifton, NJ. Starting there, I am just learning about Taking care of the pots and pans. Man, this is tough! But, in a strange way, it is fun. Yup, I said fun! There is almost nothing better than the smell of bakery in the morning or afternoon or well, whenever! Working there on the weekends was great. Especially on Sundays when the owners give me a LARGE bad or two of leftovers. Well, the unfortunate thing is that mom has decided that she and I have hypoglycemia. Low blood sugar. So, I can't have them at home. So, when dad comes by, we each grab a piece or two. When we get home, my grandparents who live downstairs get some and the neighbors get the rest. My neighbors get the rest. I enjoy working so much, I even get another job. I am now working at a small pizza place. Not a big major one, just a small one, about the size of a Dairy queen place. OK, well, maybe a little larger. I am not doing the pizza stuff though. I am making the sauce, onions and all. Man, it feels so darn good to be out of the house, going to work, maybe making a few bucks here and there. In addition, mom and I are delivering newspapers off of the back of the truck. We go to a place at about three AM, put the papers on the truck. Then we go into town and she drives slowly around town while I jump out of the back, run to a certain house and put the newspaper in the neighbors' door. Then I run back and do the next.

After school, I deliver a different newspaper to the neighbors. Almost daily. Then I go from door to door to collect the payments. OH JOY!!!

Well, maybe not really making that much you see. As part of my growing up, I am learning about responsibility. So, whenever I get paid, the money goes right to mom. I can understand it though. Hey, everyone has to pay for what they have. Whether it is rent, food, clothing or anything else, you have to pay your dues.

CHAPTER 4

Well, there has been a major change. I have been away for a while, but I don't remember too much about it. I just remember that my twin is gone away. Not died. Just away. He has nullified his part of the adoption and changed his name back to his birth name. So legally I have no brothers.

I remember that I have run away. I know that just after I have run away, my parents have bought a house in Greenwood Lake NY. My dad picks me up from some kind of runaway shelter or something like that and we drive there. It is a really nice place. A three-bedroom split level place with a fireplace downstairs and an attached garage. A small yard in front. Not much of a back yard. It seems the house is built into a hill. But **WOW!** Compared to our old house! You see, our old house had my mom's parents living in the basement and the rest was finished bungalow. A small place, that's for sure. I think is actually called a bungalow.

Greenwood Lake is the new place to us, right above the lake with some great views. Not actually on the lake itself, just on the road on top over the lake. Great views of the snow on the lake and trees in the winter and nice changing colors in the fall and easy access to the beach. Just head down the street a way and then into the lake itself. It is a nice small town with Frank's Pizza right on the road to the lake, one or two stop signs, Grand Union grocery store, one diner and about five bars! Go figure!!

The town is so small, there is only one stop light in town and one small post office. The mail is basically General Delivery Mail. Either you wait in line for your mail or you rent a post office box. A small town with neighbors and all. Not one on top of the other, a woodsy kind of town that you physically have to walk out of your house, down the street and then you can talk with the neighbor. The phone system is old too. There is nothing wrong with it. It is just that it is old. Instead of having the full seven numbers to dial, you only need five for your local calls.

My mom and I are still having problems. I think we will probably for, oh, a real long time! My dad has eventually brought home two full size dogs. Thankfully they are not the pocket ones. Neat dogs. Shep is one of their names. I forgot the other one. They don't get along too well with each other. So, they are kept on either side of the house. But hey, I get along with them both.

So now I am in a new place. Well, sort of. A new physical place, but with my parents. So now I start High School. Monroe Woodbury High School. It is a neat school. I am keeping to myself for the most part. Well, at least to start.

Like I said before, problems are restarting with mom. She is trying to write a book. (Looks familiar, eh? LOL) so I start helping by make dinner or something like that. After dinner one of my chores are to clean the dishes, pots and pans. But then, I also have some other chores. See, it seems that mom really likes ferrets and cats.

My dad uses less than one half of the garage. He and I are using the rest, as well as part of the downstairs one half as cages for mom's favorites now. Mom has over sixty ferrets and cats. Dad and I are building cages to keep the males separate from the females. One type from another. I now have to keep them fed and cleaned up. Plus taking care of the dogs, cleaning the dinner pots, pans and dishes. I must make sure that all gets cleaned up. Hey, I don't mind it too much though. Hey, it keeps me busy. But if I do not do the dishes well enough, when I get home from school, I find any not-cleaned enough dishes on my bed in my room. So now, my priorities have changed a bit for this day at least. I now have to get the dishes all washed up and put away first. Plus, now I have to make sure my bed is clean. Hey, again, at least I am keeping busy!

Unlike most kids like me, I am really starting to like going to school. I enjoy going to school because I am just getting away from my house. I am going around school, holding hands with this fantastic looking gal! Eventually we end up cutting classes occasionally cut classes. Occasionally we do get caught, but for some reason we never get detention. We are just told, "OK

Romeo and Juliette, time to get back to class". We do split up for now. Maybe for a couple of classes, but then there we go again!

My neighbors are some great people. The Hopper's. The dad is a New York City police detective or Sergeant I think. Or, well, is some kind of important guy down there! The mom is a professional nurse. Then there is Johnny Joe, two years then me, Lorraine, one year younger than her big brother, Jimmy, one year younger still and then Caroline, the youngest. A couple of years younger than Jimmy. And then there are the grandparents. They live next door to the Hopper's, like I said before, we are not houses built up next to each other. Living on Greenwood Lake gives you plenty of room between neighbors. So, John's, or as his grandfather calls him, Johnny Joe, is next door. Now, let me give a quick explanation for the name thingy: The grandfather is John Joseph, the father is John Joseph, and my friend is John Joseph. Hence the grandfather's nickname for John is Johnny Joe.

They live across and down the street from us. There are no sidewalks by us because we do not live "in town". We are about one mile or so from town. They turn out to be my saving grace place. A place to get away from home and from whatever is going on. Kind of like, well, my own little book. I can open the book, read the pages and slip right into the story. They do not seem to mind me being around their family. I do not know, even till this day, if they knew we were having family problems, but still.

They have a nice yard that goes into the lake as well as a small "private island". Nothing big, just a little bit of something that you can tie a small boat up to and maybe catch some sun in peace and quiet.

John and I get to be good friends. One day he and I were talking and he told me about this old guy in town. John likes going over to this guy's house and make some things with leather stuff. So, one day he and I head over there and we start trying the leather thing. One thing that I made was a small keychain. You see, my dad was in the Navy, my uncle was in the Navy, and one of my grandfathers was in the Army. Although I am sixteen, I had thought about it just a little bit. Not much, but just a quick thought.

Eventually I start school. All is going pretty well. Just going on day to day and getting through my classes.

I finally meet this girl, Laura. She sorts of glances my way and then me to her. **WOW!** What a knockout! I am wondering what a great looking gal like that would EVER want to be seen even acknowledging me! Eventually, we do get to know each other little by little. Then, well, we start holding hands. She starts introducing me to her friends and I am getting to know these folks more and more and more. And, well, I like it! A LOT!

School is going well. Laura and I are getting along very very well, holding hands, kissing in school and all. Occasionally we are caught by the school monitors. The thing is thou; we have never gotten any detentions or anything like that. We have been nicknamed Romeo and Juliette. Whenever we are caught, which is rare, we are just told to go to class. That's it! Unfortunately though, she lives in Monroe NY and I am in Greenwood Lake. Heck, it might as well be Timbuktu! I do not, obviously, have a driver's license and neither does she. You see, when we moved from New Jersey to New York, I did not have enough school credits. So, I had to repeat my sophomore year. Laura is in the grade above me now, the grade I should have been in.

School itself is not going too bad for me either. About my favorite class is American History by Mr. Weaver. I guess the best way of putting it is to put myself into their shoes and living my life back in 16 21. About my favorite parts of the class when we all have to get dressed up back in those times and spend a weekend out in the woods. No radios. Nothing electric. Nothing metal. Our forks and plates had to be made of wood.

I also get put on the A/V (Audio Visual) squad. I know that slot of kids thinks this is dorky, but hey, it is cool with me!

One day a traveling circus came into town. They are starting to put things up, but they decided to ask a bunch of us guys for some held. They have agreed to give a free ticket to the show to everyone that wanted to help. Well, there are SOME things that a sixteen-year-old boy, along with any of his friends, just can NOT say to! So, John, Jimmy and I go to work now. Unloading the tents, pulling on the ropes, slamming the bars into ground, we are all working out but we and can't wait to see the show tonight! Finally, it all gets done. Man, you should see this tent and the animals and all! **WOW!**

So, after all is done, we head over to pick up our free tickets. The guy that promised us the tickets decides to NOT give them to anyone! Seems that all of the work we had done for several hours was for nothing! Well, needless to say, we are a bunch of unhappy campers!

Well, the winter is coming and I want to get a job. I have been talking to John Hopper about it. He is working at a ski place, Sterling Forest just down and into the New Jersey border. He has a car and all so he talks to whomever he needs to talk to and I get a job there. I'm working in the kitchen. Cooking the burgers and franks and all. I have always enjoyed work, believe it or not.

Well, to be honest. I guess I am just not as nice a boy as I may seem, also though, my mom is not as bad either. I mean, my parents both have let me get a job. They are both teaching me about finances. Both are letting me see my friends and all. And mostly both are hearing me when I want to go on and on and on about Laura. But at the same time, though, I guess I have not been so good a boy either. I have run away at least twice. I guess I have not been as open as I should have been with them.

Plus, when I have actually needed or wanted a few dollars, I have not been up front and let them know.

Yes, I have been working at Sterling Forest and when getting paid, I have given my check to my folks. But when I needed any cash, instead of telling them anything, I have been going into the hall close into my mom's coat pocket or purse and taking a five-dollar bill or so from there. I have never told them that I wanted to keep any of my money, so we had never made any arrangements.

My mom and I are still TRYING to get along. It is difficult sometimes though. So, after ANOTHER big blow out, I decide to take a walk away. From Greenwood Lake NY to Fort Lee NJ. I am walking. It has showed a few days ago. It is not so cold, so it is not too bad to walk. I hitchhiked all the way down to see my Foster Mom. Normally it is just over an hour's drive. But I am not driving. Yes, it is cold out and I lay down for a few minutes on the side of the road under a fence. I am tired. It has been a long day and the fight with mom has been tough. The walking is a bit worse on me then I thought or worried about or anything. So, I lay down and just want to close my eyes for a few. But then again, I realize that I can't do that! Dummy! If I lay down in the cold and close my eyes, I may not be able to open them again! I could go to sleep and not wake up! So, I change my mind and get up and continue hitching again.

I get four or five rides down. Some guys and some gals, but nothing to worry about. Not a lot is talked about with me or any of the drivers. We talk about some small business and that I am having problems at home. My last stop does not get me far from my mom's house. So, I walk about the last mile or so. The sun has come out and it is actually not too bad a day out there.

Mom is away from the house. You see, even before when we all lived there at my foster mom's house, she worked. I am not sure just doing what, I am not sure. I think it is some kind of housekeeping or something like that.

I have decided to walk around my old town. See the new firehouse and the small office supply place that I use to work at as a kid. It seems like it grew a bit, but not too much. Hey, it has only been about three or four years.

Finally, she is home from work and I wait for a few minutes to get in. I go to the front door and knock. She opens the door and gives me a hug and a smile. But it is not quite the hugging that I am expecting, but all in all, it is nice to see mom and give her a hug and kiss.

She asks me about what I am doing there and why I am not at my new home with my parents, and how I got there from my old place. So, we sit down and talk about what is going on and why I left to come down. Then, unfortunately, after lunch with her, she reminds me that THEY are my parents and I should be talk with them about this. About how I feel and why I think I am feeling like this. I agree with her and on that note, away I go now. Back home to New York State.

I re-start my hitch hiking back. The weather is actually pretty nice. Not nearly as cold as on the way down, but then again, it is not the middle of the night. The trip back, only takes me a few hours. I get two rides back and quietly get home.

Well, I've made it back home, quietly make it back home and to bed. The alarm goes off and I get ready to head back to school. There is no talk and no discussion about where I was or what I did. For that matter there was no talk because I had not seen anyone between yesterday when I left and today going to school. So, off I go to school. All is just another quiet day at home. For now.

I've gone to school as a normal day. Went through classes and got on the bus to go home. Get home and turn the key to get into the house. No problems. I head down to "my room". That is, the lower level of the split ranch house. I have the fireplace for extra heat, if I need it. My one-half baths. My bed and my clothes. By now, mom and I are not talking. We barely acknowledge each other. So, down I go and mom is in the kitchen at the top of the stairs. I hear a knock on the door and mom yells from upstairs for me to get the door. So, upstairs I go to answer the door.

CHAPTER 5

I open the door and I see a Greenwood Lake Policeman there. I open the door and invite him in, as I have always been told, to be courteous and a gentleman, especially to Law Enforcement. He asks if I am Gary Wilson, JR. I confirm that I am and ask what is going on. He tells me that it is a personal nature, but that is all. Meanwhile, mom is in the kitchen at the top of the stairs doing dishes or something. Dad is in the living room. Not knowing what is really happening here, I tell the officer that I will go downstairs and wait down there for an explanation. He stops me and tells me that my mom has signed out an arrest warrant for stealing money from her purse and wallet. So, I walk back upstairs to him. He puts the handcuffs on me. I ask him if we must do the cuffing now. As everyone can see, I am not going to run or hit or anything like that. As I am being told, it is the way that things are done and yes, I do have to do it now. So, he puts them on and I get into his car and head down to the police station to get printed and all. While I am there, I meet with a lawyer. He explains to me that my mom has signed a warrant for my arrest. He says that he does NOT think there is anything that can or will happen because it is my own mother. But then, he also warns me that almost anything can happen!

I am not so sure how long I spent any time in jail, but it was...uummm... different! I do know that somehow, some way, someone did steal my sweater! **WOW!** Even in jail someone gets things taken!

Well, my dad comes by and picks me up. We've had a short conversation. He talked a bit and I tried to listen. But, obviously, was not much in a talking mood. He's explained about just why. Because they do not have a lot of money and that they think I am heading down the wrong path. There is a TV show that has spent quite a bit time being shown lately, "Scared Straight" showing what it is like to spend time in jail. So, he and mom have decided to give me a lesson.

Well, let me tell you, it DEFINITELY made an impression on me. Both with the TV show and my folks! Then he tells me that he has spoken with an attorney. His attorney has told him the exact opposite of what the attorney guy has told me! He says that he is being told that they have a good case and we can continue all and possibly go back into jail for a long time.

However, I am being told that I have an option. All charges will be dropped if I joined the Navy. I have told him nothing, but my head is yelling and screaming, "What, are you NUTS? Why in the world would I just drop all and join the service" Again, all is quiet for now and we continue home. We get inside and go inside. I go downstairs to my part of the house and he heads up to the rest of the house. I cuddle under the blankets and get some sleep.

I get up the next day and go into school. I see Laura and my friends. God, she is looking FANTASTIC! I am explaining everything that has happened for the last few days, and, most importantly, the Navy option. I've asked her what she thinks of it. And, like so many other times, she says that it is obviously up to me. I have been thinking of it all and figured that, well; maybe it is not that bad an idea.

We spend the rest of the day at school, going to some classes, skipping some and making out during others. Man, life is so great these past few months here at school!

I've gone home and have had some thinking to do. Well, so I am thinking that hey, maybe joining and seeing the world is not so bad. I have my meals taken care of, a roof over my head and a constant bi-weekly check. Plus, maybe learn a trade. Dad and I talk a bit and we have decided to go out and talk to a recruiter. So, we take a drive into Monroe, NY and sit down with the Navy Recruiters. We end up, not only talking with them, but actually signing up. I am taking the ASVAB. (Armed Forces Vocational Battery) I have just turned seventeen and I have my parent's permission to join. Everyone is asking what I want to do when I get in. I have no big idea just yet. I am told that it is OK. I can choose once I am in boot camp. I will leave school and maybe eventually get a GED instead of my High School Diploma. The Chief recruiter and my dad are talking about old times. Remembering what it was like being in the Navy during Vietnam conflict. While the two of them are talking and all, I am chatting with the two other recruiters. A girl and a guy.

Dad is about to leave and the chief is going to give me a ride home later on. So, I am just hanging around for the rest of the day. Then the Chief informs me that it is Mary's, the gal recruiter, birthday. We are all going to go to a party at the end of the day. Cool! A party! So away we are all heading out!

Well, to be honest I am not quite sure what happened! I do remember being asked what I wanted to drink. I have not really drunk before and now here I am at a drinker at all! I have had maybe a couple of beers in my ENTIRE life. However, I do remember that dad has said a few times about how much he liked his scotch and water. So, with me being the honorable son that I am, have decided to take after him. So here I go! WOW! A bit harsh on the way down, but man, I am enjoying this party! Again, I don't remember a lot of the party itself, but I do remember having four drinks! Then I remember getting into the Official Navy white van with the chief driving. He is driving and I am the only passenger. He reaches under his seat while driving and grabs a five-gallon bottle of wine out from under the seat. While driving, he is chugging down the wine!

After a while, he has decided that maybe he has had a little bit too much drinking while driving.

Maybe we should pull over. I am agreeing with him because, well, first off, he is driving a bit awkward and well, he is a Chief. So, we go down the road a little bit more and we pull over into this lot. He pulls into this small parking lot. Then, well, surprisingly enough, the lot that we pull into is right across the street from a bar! He is telling me that he knows a girl that works there and so we should go in and maybe wait to get a ride home when she gets done. So, we go inside and, well, we have decided to be gentlemen and not waste her time or anything, decide to have ANOTHER drink! WOW man, this is getting to be one fantastic day and night!

So now that it is time to head out now. His girlfriend is driving and he is in the passenger seat and I am in the back. It seems like they know Greenwood Lake. The sun is rising and the day does not seem to be too bad. Instead of driving me up to my house, I ask that I be left in town and I will make it back on my own. I figure that it would give me some time and exercise to wear off my drinks! All is cool and I am now walking home the rest of the way. I get home quietly, place my key ever so quietly into the front door and turn the key and turn. I go inside and downstairs to hit the hay. I get undressed and just barely lay down when I hear "Gary! Get up for school!" Well, needless to say, I am He comes down and I just basically ask if I can take the day off from school because I am not feeling too well. (The understatement of the year!) He gives me an OK. Then asks if I felt good enough to go into town with him. I say sure and away we go. He then decides to hit the small diner in town for breakfast. Well, considering I have never declined breakfast before, I figured that maybe I will feel a bit better once I get something down my stomach. So, in we go.

Well, I guess I over guessed the stomach thing. We get inside and we sit down. Nothing looks too good on the menu. So, I just order something small. Dad and I are chatting. I have decided to let him know what is going on. I explain that about the party, the drive and then finally the walk home. He replies, "I know. Hey, remember, I use to be in the Navy. I knew all about the birthday party and all! I heard you come in this morning."

So, we have a good laugh and the day continues. Like I have said before, dad and I always had good relationship.

The next day I head back to school. I am a bit excited, obviously, about my trip to the recruiters, the party and the drinking. Laura and I talk. She sees how psyched I am. I also explain to her that I am looking at going into boot camp around late February. I have taken the ASVAB. I have passed and now t is just a matter of time to wait. Granted, I still have to go over and get my physical next week, but hey. There is nothing that I am worried about. School and life goes on as usual. Things are still a bit tense at home with mom, but we are getting along OK. I guess knowing that I will be there just until end of next month makes things a bit easier on both parts. I do not think she is overly excited to see me go away, but with both of us knowing that I am taking such a big next step. We all know that it is the best.

Well, a couple of weeks pass and now it is time for my physical. Dad and I take a drive out to one of the military reserve offices. I check in and all goes well as I knew it would. Granted, I am not one of those big husky-built guys. But I am in shape with all of the biking and walking and running that I have done and am still doing.

With my height at 6ft 2inches and weight at 160lbs, I guess all is going well. So now I am finishing things up and my recruiter comes over to me. He has apparently come up with a situation. It seems that one guy ahead of me has either decided not to enlist or has not made it through the physical. Either way, I have the option of going in now instead of the end of February and here it is 20 January. So, I ask how long I have to figure this out. He tells me ten minutes. So, I quickly call Laura and explain to her what is happening. I ask her for her opinion and she basically tells me to make my own choice. So, a decision is made and off I head, Boot Camp in Great Lakes Illinois. Late in January and going for my first airplane ride.

The stewardess offers me some headphones so I can listen to the music. I put them on and am a bit impressed that I can actually hear and understand the music. I am listening to Johnny Cash's song "Ring of Fire". Well, I guess I am enjoying the song and the flight a little too much. The guy in the seat next to me taps me on the shoulder and just quietly tells me to "SHHHH". I guess I am enjoying things too much!

The plane finally lands and off I go. Starting my newest life!

CHAPTER 6

All of the recruits are off of the plane and we are met by a bus and some Boot Camp guys with all of their hollering and all! Oh man, this is going to be one heck of a new life! So, we all get on the bus and head out.

It is the middle of the night and we all hit our racks, beds, for the night. Tomorrow finally gets here and then everything really starts. We all go for our haircuts, uniforms and company assignments. I am in Company Zero Six Four. Again, I am not in the best shape in the world, but hey, not in bad shape at all. Again, I am weighing in at Six Foot One and around One Hundred Sixty Pounds. People use to joke around that if I stood sideways and stuck out my tongue, I would look like a zipper!!

I am doing fine with boot camp. Doing what I am told to do, when I am told to do it. Making my rack, or bed, the right way, I guess I am doing well enough with all of my stuff the Company Commander has asked me to be the company YO-YO, Yeoman, for the whole group. I have agreed. I figure that hey, if the boss asks you to do something like this, I had probably not said "No" to.

So, I am learning my cadence call and marching and all with my company along with all of my other stuff with them, like swimming and all. Granted, you might think this is funny for a sailor, but I am not doing too well with the swimming stuff. No, I am not afraid of swimming at all. I have no fear of the water and all; I am just not doing it too well. But I am passing, learning how to use my pants as a floatation device.

As you might remember, when I first went to the recruiter's office, I had not made any decision about what special training I wanted, or what or where I wanted to be stationed on. As I remember hearing from someone somewhere, it is better to be stationed on a smaller ship. If you are on a larger command, you will probably just do "whatever" kind of thing. On a small boat, though, you have a better chance of doing what you went to school for. Well, so I had chosen as my first pick, a Guided Missile Cruiser. My other choices were small ships also.

Well, now came the time again that I had the next choice. A school or training rate. If I did not choose one myself, I would automatically be chosen to go to Boatswain Mate School. Something I am not too crazy to do. "Sweep and swab and chip and paint all the do dah day!" As I had heard about what they do. So, I have made my decision. I have decided to be a Radioman. It sounded neat. Something that I thought might be interesting. And something that would be vital on-board ship. I would see the first communication in and the last to see it go out. But well, there is one thing about it though. I would need a TOP SECRET security clearance. It would take the FBI about six months to a year to do. I had explained the folks there about my problems with my adopted mom and the arrest with my mom and all. They had no problems with it and said that the Feds should have no problems either. So, I had some paperwork to fill out for them. I had to explain everything about me and my past. My father walked out before my twin and I were even born, my six months at an orphanage, eight years in a foster home, my adoption, and then everything with my adoptive home. Holy cow! Some paperwork my butt!

They had me fill out this stuff this stuff like you would not believe! So, I go ahead and fill it all out and now I guess I wait and see. I am heading back to my company to continue my training and getting ready for my graduation. It seems like these eight weeks have flown by. Again, not too rough physically or mentally, just remembering to do what they say when they say to do it. No matter what they say or when they say it.

Well, Boot Camp is about finished. We get to head out on liberty even before we take our final test! But, as we are warned, many recruits that get to go out on liberty before their finals, end up spending two extra weeks there. We still have our finals, both physical and written tests, or finals. You know what I mean.

So, a few other guys and I head out to some club or clubs. The guys and I find a neat place. It is a sort of hole in the wall place that many people know of, but not a lot of folks go to. Sounds interesting, so we all head out to this, umm, different place. We are not sure of the name because the name of the place is actually spelled out in another name on the building. I know it does sound weird, but that is just part of it! We find the place and head in. The entry room is a strange set-up. There is a lady sitting at a desk. So, we inquire about the place. She confirms all so we ask about admission. I mean, here we are now, at a building with the name spelled out sort of like in code, a lady sitting at a desk confirming all of the info, now with a strange order. She says that if we want entrance, we must make a human pyramid! So, we successfully made one. Now we are being told to collapse it. So, we start crawling down from on top of each other and the lady there stops us. She defines "collapse" for us as basically tumbling down. So, well, here we go now! Collapse it is! She then hits a switch and a black wall opens up and into this bare we all go. Everyone inside this place is laughing and clapping at us! It seems that there was a camera in the black room and we are being shown to the whole bar! Wow, this is great! So, we all head in to have our drinks. Well, I am barely seventeen, so I have, obviously, have not been to may bars or clubs, but this seems like a real neat one. We have our drinks and spend time there and all, but now it is time to head out. But where or rather, HOW do we get out? We find the exit alright. It is a slide from upstairs to the exit! So, sliding we go! Outside and downstairs now, we grab a taxi and head back to the base.

We all made it back, in one piece even! So now Monday is our finals, physical and written, so we all take some time reading and studying. Well, that is, most of us do. As Company Yeoman, I have to make sure that everyone's records are up to date, their shot records, evaluations and everything else. So, while everyone else is doing all of their studying, I am doing all of this. I am not worried though. Physically, Boot Camp was not very tough on me. I am in good shape when I came in, so I had no worries about that part. However, there was some concern about the test. I thought I would do OK, so I am not worried too much about it.

So now, Monday comes and the whole company marches down for their tests. We take them and then head back to the barracks to wait for our grades and all. Finally, the guy in charge comes back and calls out four names, mine included. Well, it seems that I had not passed. I, obviously, was not a happy camper about it! Now I have to take two more weeks of Boot Camp! So, I pack my things and go to another company. My old company, 064, was no longer mine. Now I have another one!

I am heading off now to my new company. By some sort of coincidence or something, on the same day, I get a note to make a collect call. This is weird. It is a New Jersey area code, but the number is not one that I know. I take a second look now. It is from my twin brother! Now, I am wondering how and why with many things. Why call me? How does he know

I am here? What is so important that I am told to call collect? So many questions and no answers YET!

So, I get the go ahead and make the call. David accepts the call and so we talk for a few minutes. Well, it seems that he has found our natural mother! He explains that he has found her and has found out about our past and answers some questions. He also tells me that I actually had a middle name from before. We had gone through life before as my being the only one of four boys without a middle name. It turns out that my middle name was Andrew! I was Craig Andrew! **WOW!**

David now asks me if I want our mother's phone number. Of course, I said "Yes", but at the same time, I am a bit anxious and scared to make that call. I mean, what if we talked and I could not accept any of her reason for giving us up? What if she and I talked and she did not like the one she is talking to? Me? What if? What if? What if? There are so many questions and only one way to get the answers.

The next call I made was to mom. We talked for a while. It was basically a discussion between two adults. I would ask questions and she would basically respond. No "Yes" or "No" answers, but rather explanations. We could not talk a lot or long periods, obviously, with the Boot Camp thing going on. But we talked a bit. She then surprised me with an offer. She asked if I wanted to meet her. If so, she would be willing to come up to Boot Camp graduation. I replied "Yes" and we met about a week later.

We had our Boot Camp graduation inside one of the Drill Halls for all of our families, guests and visitors to see. Well, let's just say that I am so proud to be there! The taking of that next step in life! I am happy and proud to be there. For my mom to be there! I am proud, happy and, yes, a bit scared.

After the marching and drilling was done, we all had to stay in rank until we were released and let go to our visitors. So, I waited for what seemed like forever. When finally released, everyone let go and ran up or down to find their families. I went slow and looked around, not knowing what to see or, better yet, WHO to see.

Well, then this lady shows up in front of me. Looking, well, like I was, looking around for whomever. She then approached me. I think we shook hands and we talked for a few minutes. We decided to go to the hotel room she had rented. She had some pictures of my twin and I as babies. Turns out that we were so small, she used to use handkerchiefs for diapers! Man were we tiny! We were born two and a half months premature! Baptized Baby A and I as Baby B, well, go figure! I guess we pissed off A LOT of folks by living THIS long!

We stayed together for a while, talking, asking and answering from and to the both of us. It had been just as long a time as she without us and vice versa. But we both left with some closure, in a strange way, about our pasts. Yet we both knew that neither of us wanted to give each other away again.

The next day, I received my orders. Harsh times I could tell were ahead of me, just by the orders. Going to a new place for school, Radioman "N' school in San Diego, CA! Tough duty, eh? Well, considering I had only been to New York and New Jersey all my life, except Boot Camp in Great Lakes, this is a defiant change in my life! It seems that there were some new rules in the Navy these days. When in Great Lakes and going to school on the West Coast, you do not go home on leave right after Boot Camp. You go to school first, THEN you get one or two weeks off. Then, if you are from the East Coast, you are stationed back there. Granted, just by seeing San Diego and hearing everything about West Coast, I would not have minded being stationed there, but then again, I guess you can call me an East Coast kinda guy!

So now I am off on a flight to San Diego. The flight itself does not seem to take that long. At least not to me. I am in my Navy Dress Blues. So, about the only things to be worried about are my orders in hand, my cover, and my duffel bag. All in all, not too much to worry about. So, worry was not something I had in mind. I do remember landing. The door opened and the steps were brought up to the plane. They were brought up and we walked down the stairs to the ground. All that I can say about San Diego was **WOW!!!** My first whiff at the plane's door was, I guess, tropical air! It was nothing I had ever smelt before and never have again!

CHAPTER 7

It is 7 March 1981. I get my duffel bag with all of my things and head out to RTC/NTC San Diego, CA. RTC/NTC is, as I am told, different in some ways. Recruit Training Command Naval Training Center is not all that different. The Boot Camp, RTC, has part of the base in a secluded area. They do all of the usual start up stuff, but on very rare occasions, some of the recruits come over to our mess hall for lunch or dinner or something like that. However, we are "warned" not to "mingle" with them. Hey, no problem here. I just ignore the "new pukes"!!

The base itself is real nice. The barracks are not all that different from Boot Camp. Yes, we have more room and a large closet. But to finally be free and away from all of the "Yes Sir, No Sir" and all. Plus, now we can wear civvies! So, I head out to the Navy Exchange to buy whatever we want or need. Well, I guess that makes me like most everybody else. Heading out, hitting the store, the Navy Exchange, buying whatever, smelling the sweet life and continuing with life!

A lot of new things are happening right about now. Then again, just barely turning seventeen, quitting high school and being in the Navy, I guess there is an awful lot of firsts for about anyone. I am starting Radioman "A" school finally. We have to get dressed in our "Dress Whites" for any winter and fall months, "Dress Blues" for the spring and summer months. We would have to wear them usually on Fridays. The "Undress Blues" for any other days.

During our Inspection Days we would be inspected very closely, obviously, for anything. There was one thing that I had learned in boot camp helped me out in there as well as in here: Cigarette Lighters. Thankfully, I do not grow a lot of facial hair, so shaving for me is not such a harsh thing. But I have learned is that by doing a close shave and then using a cigarette lighter close to the skin, but not "too close" is a good thing. You see, if you got caught on anything during inspection, whether it is facial hair, uniform problems, dressing problems or anything at all, you were assigned "Demerits" If you get so many demerits, you have some "Splainin' to **do!**"

While in San Diego a lot of my life both turns around and opens up. For example, the love of my life from High School, Laura, and I, had been speaking on the telephone. You see, she is the one true love of my life. She is the one that I wanted to spend my life with. Not sure if I have told her or not, but she is the one for me! Again, we have been talking and kept up with whatever I could.

While here, I have to acknowledge one thing: I have quit High School. So now I need to get my GED. I know that if I were to go anywhere or do anything, I need to at least do this then at least that part of my life, a High School diploma, has closed. So now to figure this into whatever else I have going on!

Well, soon I find out that there are other duties to do. Like standing watch for four hours at the Barracks. You would have to spend four hour duties at the front door of the barracks checking I.D's to make sure that whoever wanted to come in there was supposed to be in there. No, it was not a hard thing to do, but four fours in the middle of the nigh getting up, getting dressed and standing up outside was not one of the better things to do!

Now, please understand that I am not a guy that will go to work doing anything just so I did not have to pull duty. Nor am I a "Bible Thumper". However, I am baptized Protestant; my Foster Mom was Catholic and my Adopted Mom Jehovah Witness. I am, however, someone that does believe that there is some God out there and maybe I should be going back to Church and figure things out. Well, I find out that if you do pull duty singing in the Church Choir, both Catholic and Protestant, you do not have to pull duty! Now, I have been told that I have a pretty good voice. Granted, for one do not really thing so, but I have been told this. Plus, remembering back when I am younger with the plays and all, I figured that well, maybe it's not all THAT bad. Plus, they can just say "No" if it was that yucky! But lastly, it would be making sure I did get to church, like my Foster Mom always wanted us kids to do, but this time, I am going to two services a week, plus choir practice weekly. I guess Mom would be happy. Getting closer to God and all!

So now I go to try out for Choir. I guess it goes OK because they do not kick me out. Well, either 1) I am not all that bad or 2) they really really need people!

The Choir Director is a civilian guy. A guy that is so good, very good! He starts the practice by waving his hands through the air and singing along with all of us, abound ten or fifteen. But hold on a second, where is the music coming from? He is singing and waving his hands, but the music? OK, then I see it: his feet! He is playing the piano with foot petals! WOW! So along with the choir I go. I guess I am doing OK, however the Choir guy has other thoughts for me. He and I start talking and I have come up with an idea for the Choir, especially for the Protestant Service. You see, think there are several others in the choir that are pretty good. He agrees with me. So, we put together a Barbershop Quartet! I am singing baritone, whoever else can sing whatever else.

I guess I am not all THAT bad. I mean, well, no one threw anything at us, no one ran screaming and no ambulances were called.

So now I am, I guess you can say, somewhat successful with the choir thing. But now something else has caught my eye. At the Navy Exchange there is a back area with some real nice flowers and plants. They all look really nice. Now, please understand that I am not the flowery kind of guy. Yes, I do like the flowers, but there is one other thing pulling me this way. Naoko Kubo, the gal who takes care of the florist. I find myself going to the Exchange a bit more then, I guess you can say normal. That is, at least for my normal...

Naoko and I get started in a nice thing going on. I am spending time there and she is showing and explaining about how to care for all of the plants and all. I guess you can say that we were dating, in a light way. No, nothing like I guess that some people thing, but loose dating, like dinner, movies, holding hands, etc. I wish there was more going on, but I am very respectful of her wants and needs, regardless of mine. I am also remembering Laura from High School. I do remember that I know I wanted to wait for.

While we are talking and teaching and all, eventually we get around to talking about age. Now, please remember that I am 17, and she gives me her age. As I had been taught all of my life before: Never Ever ask a lady her age!! By her looks I know she is older than me. I am figuring somewhere around 25 or so. She tells me and I almost fall over!! 36! **WOW!** I guess you can say that, well, I guess I do go for older women!!

While stationed there, I guess I am doing some very good things, or rather, doing the right things in the right way, with one problem. For some reason I am having problems with my right arm. I have almost no feeling in my right arm, except for a thin area pass going from my elbow to my pinky. I have no idea why or how. I am not sure if I slept on it weird. I go to Sick Call to have it looked at. Now granted, in my own opinion, Navy doctors are supposed to be the best. But from what I have just been seeing with the way they are trying to find out the problem, I am not so sure.

The doctors put me on Medical Hold. Now, it is not as bad as it may seem. I am moved from my barracks to a holding place. Same basic setup, just a different location. There is not a lot that I am doing here, just some of the basic things. Plus though, I do continue the Choir. I know how important it would be to my mom, as well as to me, I guess.

Naoko and I are still getting along very well with the dating and all. But, well, there is now a change thing happening here. While on hold, I meet up with this guy. We, I guess, become buddies and all. He introduces me to this gal that he knows. It seems that there is an interest in me! Well, I do not think that I am good looking or anything at all like that! No way!! So, I tell him about Laura and Naoko and all. I explain that I am not interested in this gal. So, he starts making the moves on her, which, as you can assume, I have no problems with. All is fine here except well, when he moves in with her and then asks if I am interested in moving in too. I have thought about it for a couple of days and decided to go for it.

My arm has been taken care of. No one has found out about how or why or anything. I have gone through *PIT* (Physical Therapy or Pain and Torture!) for a few months now. I have been returned back to Full Duty. I am continuing Radioman *"A"* School. Plus, now I am going through another class: Morse code! This is a class that I have always wanted to take. Ever since I was a kid, I have had an interest! So now, things are going very well. I am back in school, going through an additional school and am about to move in to a civilian house, off the base! Everything is also going well with Naoko. But my time here in San Diego is coming to a close. I have been here for over a year now and it is time to get going. I have just gotten my orders. USS Harry E Yarnell (CG-17) out of Norfolk, VA. But before heading down there to meet her, I head home for about two weeks.

Boy I am sort of scared, sorry of happy and sort of confused.

A bit confused because my parents have moved away from the new house in Greenwood Lake, NY and back into our old house, the small one with my grandparents, my mom's parents. The only thing that I had head is that my dad, who is supposedly one quarter Indian, Cherokee, refused to pay the mortgage because the White Man owed the Indian's land that was supposedly taken. Well, if this is what he thought, well....everyone can make their thoughts.

Today's date is 10 March 1982. Well, it's not that the date is so much to remember, it is just that I have been in San Diego for one year and three days. Man, what a great time! I had learned so much about this thing called life. About what it is like to make the right decision. As well as being aware of situations if you do NOT make the right one!

Chapter 8

So now, I get back home and see everything for myself. **WOW!** Talk about shock! I had heard about my dad having a heart attack, but **WOW!** This is a man that would pick up a train battery, about two hundred pounds, with one arm, put it on his shoulder and carry it to wherever. Now this giant has gotten so thin and frail. He has gone from six feet tall, about two hundred and forty pounds to about six foot, one hundred and thirty pounds. My leave, time off from the Navy went OK. Mom and I do get along for a while together, but not too much. Dad and I have always gotten along somehow, someway.

Well, it's time to get the heck out of dodge, as my dad would say. Heck, he is from Illinois, so I listen, and grow to like, country music. So, Dad gives me a ride to the airport in New York City. WOW! This place is humongous! With all of the people and planes! I do not think I could even imagine this place!

I look at my orders. They are telling me to fly out to Sicily so I can meet up with my ship, USS Harry E Yarnell. I cannot wait to get going on and continuing this trip called life. I get to the counter in uniform, hand over my duffel bag, keep my orders in my hand and get ready for takeoff. I'm not sure how long the flight is out there about I REALLY do NOT care! I have my orders, my packed duffel bag and some cash. Life could not get any better!

We finally land in Sigonella, Sicily. Heck, this Navy thing is not so bad. I have just spent a couple of months in Boot Camp, met my natural mother, one year in San Diego, dated an "Older Woman", Naoko, learned a new trade, Communications, a second school, Morse Code, and now flying, FREE, to Europe. Not a whole lot of messes!

So, now I am on TEMPDU, Temporary Duty, in another country. No, there is nothing wrong with that, I am just put in Temporary Duty barracks. I just have to spend some time doing Boatswain Mate things. Pick up garbage, mow the lawns and clean the heads. Hey, I figure that I can live with it. And that is what I do. Hey, it is not like I am losing anything. I mean, that, well, I have not really done anything in my trade! Bu I am anxious. I mean, I have spent time going through school, getting my TOP SECRET security clearance, or at least having the FBI work on it still. (I have heard that it can take up to one year to get it all done!) I guess you can say that I am one of those low life kinda guys. No, not the kind that causes trouble and leaves, but the guy that just always keeps in the back. Not causing problems, not brown nosing and not yelling or screaming, just the guy that goes on day to day.

Well, I guess I can say that I am a nice guy, except, well, let's just say that I am learning every four-letter word. I learned to swear as much as I wanted to anyone I wanted. If I did not want them to know what I said, I did it in a different language! In Sicily, I swore in English, to any of the other guys on duty with me, I swore in Sicilian. Either way, I got my point across!

So, here I am spending about two weeks in Sicily doing whatever needs to get done, surprisingly to some of the guys there, getting upset that I am not onboard my ship. Well, I guess some of these folks, who, granted, have been in the Navy longer then me, consider this a sort of vacation.

Now, everyone has heard about Pizza and Italy and all. How they both go hand in hand. I knew I had to at least try it. I mean, hey, I grew up in New Jersey visited New York City once or twice. Believe me, I know pizza! At least USA Pizza! The base is not in the middle of town or anything like that. So I went to the pizza place on base where they have the locals cooking and all. So, I head out and get some pizza. I am so psyched! Imagine, **WOW!** Here I am, in Sicily, going to have some homemade Italian food! So I order a whole pie because I do not want to try just a piece from someone else's pie. I want my own fresh made pizza. If I don't eat the whole thing, in which I know I probably won't, I'll take the rest to go and either pass it out to my friends out here or, heck, maybe I'll just keep it for myself!!

So now, I order it with sausage. Nothing real big, just a regular one with sausage. I get it and take a crunch. Well, to be open and honest with you, I am, to put it nicely, very disappointed in it! The crust is thin and, instead of sauce, they are using tomato slices! So I eat a slice and give the rest to the other guys. I can say that I am definitely not the only guy that feels this way!

I am just in a limbo mode. Hey, I have spent so much time and the government has spent so much money sending me to school and flights all around the place! I just want to get where I belong and not in this limbo! Granted, Sicily is neat and the language is easy, at least for me, to learn. Now I just want to get out of here and on board my ship and get to duties!!

Well now, I guess someone heard me somewhere! I just received notice that I now have to go to Naples, Italy to catch up with my ship now. I have no idea how or why Naples comes into play. But I guess that is why they are called "Orders". They say to go and away I go! Packing my duffel bag up with all of my uniforms and all, as Jackie Gleason use to say, "Away we go!" Maybe not WE, but ....but I am sure that you get the point!

I am now on a dual prop small plane going from Sigonella to Naples. Granted, I have not been flying a lot in my life, but boy, this does look like a small plane! The flight is about an hour long. We land and all is good. Well, so I thought. I am now being told that I was sent up here in error. Seems that tomorrow I am being sent BACK to Sigonella! I am not going to get upset or pissed or anything like that. Hey, as I have been told, getting mad and throwing your temper around gets nothing done. It will probably just make matters worse! Well, I guess that now I can say that I have actually put another, not many so far, knick in my holster!

So, now I am heading back to Sicily on that small little puddle jumper. Again, I am not afraid of it or anything like that. It is just another day.

I have landed back now and so I get back to the same place, same area, and same racks. Thankfully, though, I am back here for just a few days. My next stop, I am finding out is Rota, Spain.

OK now, let me see if I have it all together: I quit High School at 1 7, joined the US Navy, went to Boot Camp in Illinois, spent a year in San Diego, CA going through Radioman "A" school and then Morse Code School, applied for, and got, I assume, TOP SECRET security clearance by the FBI, flew to Sicily, then to Italy and back to Sicily just to find out that I am now going to Spain. **WOW!** I guess you can say that it has been an interesting year or fifteen months so far. All of this, and I STILL have not met up with my ship!

I am now off to Rota, Spain. All of these flight and trips and all just, I guess it proves that I am not afraid of flying!! So now I have just landed and am getting ready, AGAIN, to be put in this transient position thing, AGAIN! Here I go. Assigned to my temporary place and await my orders. I figure that I will probably be either in the laundry area or the grounds keeping. But either way, I figure, that it is just temporary.

As a new arrival, temporary or not, we are all given a briefing or setup of the rules of the base, the base is basically Spain's. The United States just sort of has some property there. The largest thing is that we are all being told to watch and obey ourselves and be proper and courteous to the base folks as well as out in public. Well, there is no problem there. Heck, I am always brought up to be respectful to all. Then they bring up this one' "sensitive".

It seems that there is one area that we have to be very careful. We are told that if, while in the area were ordered to "STOP", we had better do just that! The Spanish police are told that they can order the stop once. If you do not stop, they have orders of basically shoot to kill! Great! I don't speak a word of Spanish and I could get shot! No concerns here! LOL

After being there on the base for a day or two, I decided to head out for the night and, well, be a Navy guy! The only clothes I had access to were my Navy Dress Uniform and my Navy Dungarees. Well, being that I could not leave the base in my Dungarees, well the only option was obvious. So, I get dressed and head for a walk into town. Alone, but I am not concerned though. Hey, the base is the base is the base. Downtown was right there. So, I head out. I am hitting this one place right there, nor far from the base. Seems like an OK kind of place. I order myself a drink. It is a local drink. Not too bad. I have the drink and look around. Not a lot happening here, so I have decided to leave this place and head out for another one.

I head down the block to yet another one. Seems cool here too, but at least I am not the only guy in there. So, this other squid, Navy term, and I chat for a while with the bartender. So, I've ordered me a local drink from this place now. Not too bad! I make myself all comfortable at the end of the bar because the other guy just left and the bartender and I start talking. I am a bit surprised though. He speaks very good English. So, we talk for a few. Some other customers come in and he handles them. Well, I take a look at my watch now. It's getting up there. I have had four or five of these drinks and I seem to be doing OK with them. I mean, they do not seem to taste like heavy alcohol. So, now I get up and WHAM! Almost hit the floor! Like I say, ALMOST! I catch myself with my arms and I re-set myself. After a few minutes I try this getting up and walking thing that I had learned so many years ago by my mother! Well at least now, this time all appears to be going well.

I am now leaving the bar and heading back to the base. The only thing going through my head just now is worry. I am worried that I may not hear the Spanish police tell me to stop. Worried that I appear to be just some drunk guy that has made it onto this base! All of these worried things, until that is, when I get back to the barracks. AAHHH! Now safe and sound. Now just to figure out how I am going to get into my rack, bed. It seems that me, being over six feet tall. Somehow, I am dealt the top rack place. So now I have gotten up to bed and am all at rest and peace.

Until wake up! The lights turn on; the guy in charge throws a metal garbage can down the middle of the room while yelling and screaming "WAKE UP". I jump up so fast I forget I am on the top bunk and hit my head on the low ceiling and pipes! OH MAN! What a way to get up after drinking last night!

I manage to get up and all. Make my way to grab a shower and get dressed and breakfast and then just get on with my day. That is, with a hangover! So now I am just sitting under the trees, with a throbbing headache, and hoping and praying that I will get something easy to do. I finally get my assignment and I get to that. Not real hard, just working outside. Some shade, some sun. All in all, not too bad, I guess. Besides, I find out, I am going to meet up with my ship! FINALLY!

CHAPTER 9

Finally, I get to her. WOW! USS HARRY E YARNELL (CG-17) A guided missile cruiser. A crew of around four hundred and fifty, a real ship! Giving me the opportunity to really serve my country just like I have been hoping and dreaming and training for.

I get onboard and am assigned my rack. The bottom rack in the radioman's quarters plus one half size locker to hang up my dress uniforms. The rack is different. The top half, with the mattress and all, lifts up and everything else goes into there.

I am informed that, because we are radiomen and communications has to be up and running twenty four hours a day, seven days a week, we are on our own schedule. So when we hear about "swapping shifts", it does not apply here. When we pull into port in a foreign country, like Spain, which is where we are now, the ship is shut down. So we are tied up to port, change power from ship power to docking power and receive stores and supplies and all of that good stuff, we still have to have communications up and running like we are underway. The watches for radiomen in port or twelve hours on and twenty-four hours off and the underway sift are six on and six off. Not bad, eh?

Well, I have just gotten on board and am ready to roll! I am told to get changed and put on my dungarees so I will get a quick tour of the Communications Station and where some of the other equipment is located on board. For example, where some of the transmitters and receivers are located. As I am told, for "just in case" transmitting for help, etc.

Well, by now it is time to get underway. I get the combination to CommCent. I get my assignment and am getting ready to go! We get started. We are underway and am not feeling too well. Oh my God! I cannot believe it! Here I am, seventeen years old, a volunteer sailor in the United States Navy and am seasick! Because I am so sick, I am relieved of my duties, but not going to my rack to sleep it off or anything like that. Instead, I am assigned to stay in the radio shack on the floor with a bucket. Believe me, in a weird way, I can almost understand this. Hey, what good am I going to be to anyone sleeping or getting sick in my rack? At least with me sticking it out up here, I am not getting away with anything. I am still stuck "on duty".

Well, thankfully this thing only lasts a day, about twenty-four hours. After the next day, all goes well. I am now running around ship. Doing whatever duties were needed, going out on deck feeling and smelling the great sea air and sea salt. It is ten fantastic days!

We finally get home. But, well, it is a different style of home. My new home is on board the Yarnell.

While in port, my chief has been going through my records. I guess he likes what he is reading and calls me into radio central to have a brief meeting. In a way, I am a bit scared. Does he want to tear me down for getting sick while underway? Did I do something wrong?

The chief sits me down and we talk about the usual stuff at first. Then asks me what I want from the Navy. I basically tell him, "basically, whatever I can get out of it". Whatever classes I can take, whatever I can learn". I guess he likes what he hears from me because, well, he is sending me to school! Again! No, not Radioman's "A" school, but one that is being pulled back now. I am one of the last guys going through this. I am going to "Safe Cracking School"!

I'm told that this school is being pulled back little by little. It seems that some of the guys that have gone through this as, well, used this training for their own "personal" use. They have been teaching fewer and few guys and fewer and fewer ways. But, well, here I am! Willing to, as I told my chief, learn more and more!

Basically, because all of our information so classified and is kept in safes, like our TOP SECRET codes and all, there are times that if something happens and we cannot get into the safes via normal means, there should be an alternate. So, I guess I am it!

It turns out that the school is right there on base. So, I get my orders and head to class. It is a week's school right there on base, like I said, but I need orders to go for it. I get to stay on board my ship and I just commute.

Well, I guess it turns out good that I have gone to this class. I have just graduated, successfully I might add, about a month ago and well, for whatever reason, and we cannot get into our safe, so I am called in. I take my tools and go into the crypto room. I cannot let anyone else see what is going on, so behind closed doors, I am set to work. I do all my wonderful things and "POOF". The safe is now "magically" opened, boy, is everyone glad there was someone around to do this. Otherwise, am not quite sure what would happen, but I do not think it would be pretty!

One of my other duties on board ship is raising and lowering the aft antennas for helicopters. Whenever a helicopter has to "swing by" to pick u or drop off anything urgent, the aft antennas have to be lowered so they, obviously, do not get caught up with the helicopters.

I am on the radio shack doing my duties and I hear something through the grape vine. It seems that one of the enlisted crew has just had, I guess you could call it, a bad day! He has confronted the Captain about the Captains duties on board.

He inquires, "What does the Captain do on board ship?" The Captain replies "Well, I Captain the ship and am in charge, and responsible, for whatever happens on her". The enlisted man inquires, "From where?" The Captain replies "From the bridge". So then the enlisted asks, "Then why don't you have your ass on the bridge in charge of this place instead of standing here talking to me!?!?!" (Well, he has used some other words, but I will try to be nice!)

The next I am called down to lower the antennas because a helicopter is being called in to medivac this seaman out!!

So now, all is going well. I am over my sea sickness, working as a regular radioman, being a regular sailor. Now, this is something I am very proud of!

We are finally pulling back into part, Norfolk, VA, the largest Naval base in the world I am told. Not just the United States, but anyone anywhere. All is still going well. Man, though, it is different living off of a ship. I mean, with the way you keep your clothes, the way you wash your clothes, the way you keep an eye on all of your things. Granted, for the most part, everyone is cool. I mean everyone is not trying to steal everything from everyone. But it is just a few that messes it up for so many others. I try to keep on every ones good side. So whenever grandma sends some of her home made chocolate cookies and brownies I share them with anyone/everyone else. Grandma is used to sending these things out. She had been doing it for dad and Uncle Lin when they were both in Vietnam as well as, occasionally, for my unadopted twin brother. Man, can grandma bake!!

Well, it's time to get underway again! We are heading to Europe again. Finland, Denmark and England. This is not a bad thing. Like is said, "Join the Navy, See the World"! I'm a bit concerned about my getting seasick. I think so is the chief and all. Granted, I do not think that it is a big concern. I mean, there have got to be others! The longest I have been underway is ten days. I guess we shall see!

We are getting underway, that's for sure! Yup, it's happening again! Thankfully, this is only for a day or so. After this, all is good! I can eat at chow times, sleep whenever and be a regular guy. While underway, the Radioman's shift, like I said before, was different from everyone else. This is a good thing though. We have our schedules and the ship has hers. One strange thing, I guess you can say, is that here it is in August and we are running around in pea coats. Because of all of the sensitive communications equipment there, we have to keep our own air conditioners on. So, while it is over one hundred ten degrees in the engine room, we are shivering and shaking upstairs!

A lot of the crew wants to be our friends. You see, one of the things that we get onboard is AFRTS, Armed Forces Radio and Television Services. The crew knows about these, as well as the Red Cross messages from family to them. Each of the crew wants to be the first to get these things from us. So, they are each trying to set up something for us. The cooks try to set up a deal that if THEY get to see them first, they will make someone the BEST and BIGGEST steak around. The Electronics Technicians promise to fix or get us something. The Machinists promise to fix our car first as soon as we get back. Something for something. That's what everyone here is playing!

While underway, when not pulling our shift work, there are other things that need to get done. One example is UNREP: Underway Replenishment. We have a supply ship run up alongside of us and shoot a couple of lines from them to us, we pull the lines over and either stronger lines or fuel lines are attached. We pull whatever across and so starts our replenishment. Again, we radiomen are on our own shifts, but we also know that we have a responsibility to our crew. So, we do whatever is necessary for the storage, etc. After a couple of hours doing this, all is secure and traveling our operations continue. We are now en route to Helsinki, Finland. As I am told, though, this is a bit of a different port with one difference; we must wear our Dress Blues for the entire stay. You see, most places that we go to, we wear our dress uniforms on the first day in port. After that, we can wear our civies after. Hey, that's OK. No problems with about anyone. We pull in, get all dressed up and hit the town! One of my friends from ship, though, decide to do something a little bit different. We want to see what it is like in town to be a Finish guy in town. Not going to see anything special, maybe just hit a movie or something. So, that is just what we do! We hit a movie theater and go see a movie, "Caligula". It is funny though, seeing an American film, but Finish subtitles! Wow! This is definitely strange, but fun.

Man, that movie was different. We had never heard of the movie before and now we know why! Not for the young at heart! So now we have seen this part and the three or four of us go on and do whatever else regular folks do until tomorrow night when we head out again.

We head out to one of the clubs. There are five of us at this one club just hanging around in a small group talking and drinking until I feel a tap on my shoulder. I turn around and see the very cute looker gal (believe me, I use this term loosely!) behind me. I ask "Yes?" She asks me if I would like to dance. I am a bit taken aback and ask her "Huh? Me?" She replies, "Yes would you like to dance?" Well, I warn he "Well, sure, but I am not a very good dancer". She says that she has no problem with that. So, off to the dance floor we go! "WOW" I am saying to myself. "Is THIS what it's like to be in the Navy? Travel and women and all?!?!?" Well, let's just say that I am a very happy camper! So, we out to the dance floor we go! She sees that I am not very comfortable, so we decide to take a break from dancing and head over to our own private section of the dance room and we talk and drink for a little while. I am   not   use,   to   be honest with you, to being with a woman. I have not been with a girl yet. And, well, I still have Laura from high school, on my mind. So, I end up leaving her to find her friends and I head out to either find mine or just to head back to the ship.

I make it back now and get ready for my shift. We are there in Finland for four days and now is about time to head out and get ready for our next stop: Copenhagen, Denmark. We are on our way and, well, quite unfortunately, the sea sick thing starts in again. It seems that whenever we are on land, I have no problems, obviously. When are underway eventually I am fine. It is just that day or so when we first get going. YUCK! It is only about a five-day trip or so. Eventually all is cool though.

We are getting ready to pull into port, but we must call ahead to the police. Seems that not all folks are excited about us being there as we are. They are holding signs "NATO out of Denmark and "Yankee Go Home". The police come and clear things up. It is not a fierce and wild group. Just seems like a bunch of folks like at home, under the First Amendment, The Right to Congregate.

I know that this is not the United States, but Danish people have many similar rules and laws as we do.

All is now cleared and we pull up and get ready to hit the beach. This is great. The towns people, for the most part, are either happy to see us sailors or are just not as upset as the folks on the piers.

The small stores in town are bringing their products on carts and bringing them out to the town to show and sell their things. And man, what great things they have! The sweaters are fantastic and thick. The pottery is great too. I am buying the sweater for myself and, well, I figure I will get some coffee cups to send home to mom.

But now I am noticing something different. Seems that everywhere I look I see small golden mermaids on the ground. This is interesting. As I look around a bit more, I see a large statue. I take a look and now all is clear! Between the statue and the mermaids, I see that the statue is Hans Christian Anderson. The kids story teller. Someone we use to watch on TV every year. Some of his most liked stories were The Little Mermaid and The Ugly Duckling. We are there for five days here and now it's time to head back and go for our last stop on this route: London, England.

We arrive in Bath, England. Seems to be a nice not-too-large a town. Thankfully, this is not a dress-down port, unlike Finland. In Finland, we had to wear our uniform at all times, where as in England, just for the first day.

Getting there, we had an option: If we wanted t head out and see places, we could take a bus ride to Paris if we wanted, or a ride into London. As a Radioman, we had different hours for duty. The ship had to stay in communications, obviously, at all times. So, when we pulled in, the mechanical guys could do whatever to the boat when she was shut down. Our shifts were six hours on, twelve hours off. While on these hours, I decided to take a run into London.

I do not remember how long the ride was, but I do remember seeing the rolling hills. Granted, there were many of them, but the colors were different from home. I mean anywhere home, just a different color green. Not sure how to describe it, but just different. While going for a ride to see London, we take a stop to see one other thing that tourists come from all around the world to see, Stonehenge. The area with the stones is remarkable! Not just the stones themselves, but when you compare the stones, their size and the ground! **WOW!** London itself is neat also. It is a clean town. I have not been to New York City as yet, so I cannot compare the two, but it seems to be a cool size place with plenty to see and do in town. Plus, well there are the police in town, or to call them properly, the Bobbies or Constables. All appearing proper and set up nice and proper without guns. However, they do have their sticks, so watch it!

We all head in and ready to scram. So, well, off we go now. I guess we are doing some kind of taking our time. It is taking us about four days or so to get there. No, it is not that far, but we are just doing operations to keep busy until we get there.

We finally get back home and all is well. Between now having a cruise under my belt and getting back home, all seems to be going well, that is until I run into a situation with a "low life" on board ship.

You see, I have never touched and illegal drug even once in my life. That may impress some people, but I am not trying to impress anyone, just being open and honest. There is someone on board that decided one day that, I guess, he is low on cash, so, he asks me if I want to buy a joint from him. I obviously decline, and I go on with my job. A few days later, he sees me on the back of the ship, the forecastle, and he comes up to me and starts a conversation with me. I am trying to keep my distance, so after him saying "YO" to me, I decide to step away. He follows me and, again, asks about my buying a joint. Again, I replied "No thanks", and go on. Later on, again, he sees me and asks, almost demands, that I buy on. Again, I decline. This is getting to be a royal pain! You see, the way I look at it, is that if someone asks me once and I decline, and it's cool. The second time, well, OK. Now, the third time is a royal pain in the butt! You see, if someone decides to ask such a request and I decline each time, and the guy continues, he is either has such a damaged brain due to the drugs or is just that hard up and is willing to do anything to support his habit. And I am not crazy to have this person on my ship! You never know who you might need to rely on or what they might do to the ship!

Understand one more thing: The reason I do not take the joint is, obvious. I just don't want one. However, there is an additional one. You see, with my TOP SECRET clearance, I have to make sure I am clean at all times. If I had to take a urine spot check, and they found the pot in my system, I lose my clearance and job! So, if I decide to do anything after the Navy, I am screwed.

After the third time he has asked me, I decide to do something about it. I go to NIS, Naval Intelligence Service, now known as NCIS, Naval Criminal Intelligence Service. I explain to them what is happening. I have decided not to go to anyone on board ship because I do not want to get caught up in the middle of anything, like if someone else buys and ends up blaming it all on me.

So, I speak with one of their agents and let them know what is going on. He has asked me three times to repeat the story and inquired about if I had bought before, either from him or anyone else. He has brought the Agent in Charge into the office and I have to tell HIM now. So, here I go AGAIN. Well, now they have asked me if I wanted to or be willing to buy from him. I've said that I am not too crazy about it because I just have not done it before and I am not sure what the right way is. I mean, what if I do not use the right wording or say the right thing. You see a have a certain allergy. I am allergic to LEAD! Especially if it is not wanted to be ingested by me! We've talked for a while more and finally I agree.

So now, the next time he asks me about buying a joint, remember, this is his fourth time that he's asked, I tell him "Sure". You see, if he does, I am setting up a meeting with him. I will meet with NIS before to make sure all goes well.

So, as usual, he asks and we set up a date and time. We leave and go our merry ways, him to wherever he goes and me back to the ship, but to a phone first. (Remember, this is around 1983. Cell phone? What's that???)

Before meeting to buy, I am meeting up with NIS. They put me down to make sure I have nothing on me and get ready to send me on the way, that is, after explaining things to me and giving me a pen. You see, the pen is just a small transmitter, designed that, when pulled out of my pocket, it will let them know that all is done. But before I use it, I have to come up with a code to let them know I am finishing up. That is now all done so away I go! I make the buy, use my code and remove my "pen". About five or six agents surround us with guns drawn! They arrest both of us. I am told to get mad at the seller, to make it look like I am just as shocked as he is, this way, he will not know for sure what is going on. So now we are arrested. I go into one car with handcuffs on and he into another. Finally, they remove the cuffs and head back to the office with the agents to help with their report. They write everything down and I read the whole thing. Now they just have me initial parts of their report and I head off and back to my ship. Everything seems to be going as normal to everyone else...that is...for a week or two.

While in port, the ship and crew do things to and for the ship to keep her up and running and reliable. We also do mock operations. This time, we are tied down next to another ship for a while. The other ship is between us and the pier. While on board, we, again, do mock operations. They call over the ship, "this is a drill, and this is a drill. All hands man your battle stations." So, ahead to Radio Central I go. About ten or fifteen minutes later, there is someone buzzing at the door. Someone opens it and I am told to go outside to the hallway, or deck. I head out and the Chief Personnel man meets me out there. He hands me a package with a new set of orders. So, when no one can see or hear me because everyone is locked down, I am told to head down to berthing, (racks) and pack my sea bag totally and completely. I am told that no one, including the Chief, really know nothing, but I am to leave the ship. Permanently. I totally understand what is going on. I mean, it does not take a rocket scientist to figure this out. It seems that the guy that I bought the pot from was about to be arrested and go to Court Martial. I have to take away for my own safety and all. If the rest of the crew found out that I was a snitch, man, my head would be doing some heavy duty rolling!

So, I am now heading for Naval Air Station Norfolk, Va. I head there to may new assignment, a Navy Legal Office. Not at big as Navy Legal Service Office, just a small branch dealing mostly with contract inquisitions, etc. Nice small office, just a Lieutenant Commander boss, First Class Legal Petty Officer, 2 civilian clerks and little ol' me. Not bad.

I start working in the Legal Office and, actually, get to enjoy it! I mean, I never realized how many ways people interpret if, and, too, also and but. Well, it seems that I am actually enjoying learning all about this stuff called "law".

Easter weekend is coming up and the office is getting ready for an extra-long weekend. My boss the Lieutenant Commander, has decided to make it a full four days off. So, naturally everyone the small office, including, me, are all happy campers! I have decided to fly home to New Jersey for the long days off. My boss has decided that, for a just-in-case matter, I would have the days taken as actual Leave.

So, in case anything might happen, all bases are covered. If I return back OK, she would just tear the papers up. Well, if I did not know any better, looking back, she must have been clairvoyant in a past life!

I have flown home with no situations happening of course, just me in my civies, a bag with some clothes and, of course, my leave papers. Dad picks me up from the airport and we are heading home. We start talking and joking and having a good time on the way to the house. Not bad, but it is over an hour or so.

Well, now I am back home with my folks and grandparents and we are all actually getting along real well. My dad is a bit like Mc Gyver. He can make anything out of nothing at all. He can also build anything also. For example, there was a time a real long time ago when he needed a table saw. He did not have one, so he built one...out of an old wooden table! He took the table, cut a hole in the top, mounted a motor underneath, took a long wire and put an on/off switch on it, and ta-da!! One new table saw!!

My mom had a thing for animals, like I, and most of you have. Except, well, she took it further then many people. For example, as a kid, we had de-scented skunks, Flower and Blossom, two girls that lived in our bathroom under the bathroom sink. They were cute, de-scented and potty trained with litter sand in boxes under the sink. They also had personalities. So, you had do make sure you did not piss them off too much. When I did for the first time, I was bitten! Right through the fingernail!

Anyway, she also had a thing for ferrets. She had, I think, around thirty or so. Eventually she had the sense to keep them out of the house. My folks have a very large garage with separate doors on it; however, it was not used as a regular garage. Yes, well, one side was. It was used as working garage that my dad and grandpa used to cut wood and metal and whatever else. The also stuck whatever else they needed for anything else. The other side was for my mom's animals.

So now, this one day, my mom was working with the ferrets and my dad is helping her by building and mending their wooden cages. He looks at his watch and realizes he has to leave for work. I have been, as usual, helping him in the garage and my grandfather is outside watching us. My dad says, "I have to get going to work, Gary. Would you mind finishing this up for me?" Of course, is reply "Sure" and he heads out for work.

I turn to the infamous table saw, grab the wood, and check the wood for marked measurements. All is good so far. I get ready to make the cut and grandpa grabs onto the wood to hold it yelling over the motor "I've got it". Well, he sure does! As he grabs the wood, my hand is thrown into the saw!

Now, I am not sure how or anything like that, but I know I heard someone in the front of the driveway yell something. But I am just standing there looking at my hand, out in the driveway now, leaning on the garage looking at my hand saying "Hey... **WOW**...Check it out!!" My mind/body has already started to go into shock. Looking at my hand, of course, the wound is open and I am bleeding. I am starting to realize a little bit of what is happening here.

The index finger is the most severely damaged. It is not totally severed; it is leaning backwards though. The middle finger has also been hit and is bleeding a bit, along with the ring finger. The ring finger was just barely been hit, with just one cut on the top but inside the finger.

I guess someone has called for an ambulance, but it has not arrived yet. So, my neighbor got some large towels and drove me to the hospital. Saddle Brook is not a small tow, but not very big either. It takes us around, as I heard later that it took less than ten minutes to get there. Not a bad drive, eh? In we walk into the Emergency Room. They are playing cards there. A slow day, I guess. So, my neighbor comments to them, "Looks like you have some good hands there! But when someone gets a chance, my neighbor here almost cut off his thumb. Can someone get a chance, could you take a look!" Man, I do not think I had ever seen folks jump so quickly!! They jump up to assess my hand. After a while, they realize that Saddle Brook is too small and they are not equipped to handle my situation. So, they dope me up with pain shots, because they do not have a nurse to ride with me, put me in an ambulance and run me to Bellevue Hospital in New York City. Soooo AWAY WE GO!!!

We are doing well, going lights and siren and hit the hospital. I am wheeled in and I can still remember seeing this gal, sitting on a gurney saying, "I was here first! Why are you taking him?" Anyway, I am heading in and all is finally done. The doctors put me under and start their "fun stuff". I do remember waking up and seeing my folks standing next to me along with my old girlfriend, Laura. She and I kind of laugh at the whole thing. I mean, what good does crying or yelling do? I guess I am in the hospital for a few days but finally get the OK to leave and head back to Norfolk Air Station.

I finally get back and speak with everyone in my office. Remember the reason I am there though. Remember the guy trying to sell me pot? His case comes up and I am called to testify. So I go on the stand, am sworn in, and answer all questions, make whatever statements needed and tell everyone what happened. His Court Martial is over now. To this day, I never knew what he got or where he went or for how long.

Finally, I am through with this court stuff and I am getting transferred for Light Duty for six months. I take a look at the orders: NRTF Annapolis MD.

Naval Radio Transmitting Facility, Maryland. Wow! Right next the Naval Academy. Now I board a bus for there. I take the bus, not too super long, and then a taxi to the base. Well, it turns out that this is a high security base that is kept very quiet. The taxi driver has to ask two folks about it. Honestly, I am feeling a bit cautious. I figure that, actually, this guy is probably taking me on a ride for some bucks! So I just tell him to get there NOW or I'm scramming his taxi. I think he got my point! I get to the base finally. Man, talk about a small base. Not a lot to it. I check in with the OOD, Officer on Duty. She directs me where the barracks, uumm, rooms, are. You see, their barracks are just rooms. Each room has two folks sleeping there. Top bunk and bottom bunk. There is no show hall. The place is too small for that. So, everyone gets an extra fifty dollars a month to go grocery shopping. The command has a big enough kitchen for two or three people to cook in for themselves.

So, I get into my room and am told to hurry up and get changed. They're having a beach party outside! Of course, I think I got changed in about thirty-five seconds! I head down to the party and everyone is having a blast! Wow man ... I have a feeling that duty here is going to be real tough! HAHAHA. We are all having a blast. I have a thing for raw clams and oysters. So, I reach down into the water, grab a clam, borrow someone's knife, open it and swallow it raw and whole! A couple of folks looked at me like I am half nuts! But the rest of them realized exactly what I am doing!!

The hours for duty there are very strange. They go as two, two, two and eighty. You see, first you do two-day watches from seven am till three pm. Then when you get off at three, you go back on at eleven pm till seven am. You do the eleven pm to seven am twice. When you get off at seven am, you go back on at three pm. You do the three pm till eleven pm twice. But the good thing is that when you get off of your second shift at eleven pm, you have eighty hours off! Three days off is almost a cool payback for all of the strange hours on!

The hours are a bit strange for me, though. Remember that I am on light duty because of my hand. I occasionally have to take strange hours off and go to the Bethesda hospital occasionally to get my hand checked. The doctors there seem to be very happy with what the doctors at Bellevue have done, plus, with the way that I have been caring for it, keeping it clean with no infections and all. The hand, my right hand, which is weird because I am right-handed, seems to going cool with my using it and not under or over using it, for a while. So, the doctors there decide to give me full clearance back to full duty. Some folks might not be too happy going from a light command to a "normal" one, but I happen to be very happy getting back on this thing called life. So, I finally get my new orders. USS Exploit (MSO 440) out of Newport RI! Wow! From one great command in Maryland to Rhode Island. Sweet!! So, off I go again! Now, let me see, in the Navy for about three years. Going from Boot Camp in Illinois to school in San Diego, a Guided Missile Cruiser in Norfolk VA, to Naval Air Station Norfolk VA to shore station Naval Radio Transmitting Facility in Annapolis MD now to Newport RI. Talk about a lot of running around. But hey, I am not complaining!

I have decided to take a week or so off, so I go home back to New Jersey to see my folks and let them know how my hand is going. After a week, I decide to take the bus to Rhode Island. My dad gives me the ride to the bus station, and we joke around that he seems to be "Dads Taxi", well at least for my military time. Actually, I think that he is proud of me for joining, granted, not too happy under the original circumstances with mom and all. But all in all, he appears so.

Anyway, I get on the bus and we head out. With all of the other people on the bus, one guy sits on the seat next to me, a good-looking guy looking about my age. We start talking about my being in the Navy and what he is doing. Turns out that he is trying to be a professional male model. He is just starting out, but he shows me quite a few pictures of him. Turns out that he too is going to Newport, or rather, going back to Newport. Again, he is just starting out and has just found an apartment in town that he is going to room at with some guy that has lived in town all his life. After a while we finally reach town and we exchange addresses. He is just moving back into town, so he has no telephone number and, of course, neither do I. So, we part our ways.

I get to my ship/boat, turns out that the Exploit is a Mine Sweep. One hundred and seventy-two feet long and made completely out of wood! I get onboard the ship and hand in m orders. Seems kind of strange to me to be calling this a ship when I am used to the Yarnell.

Anyway, I get on board with my duffel bag and ask where the racks, beds, are so I can get squared away. I am told that the ship actually has two places. You see, Newport is actually a cool size command with barracks for the base personnel...and the Exploit crew. So, when we get underway for games or operations or anything at all, we have our beds, racks, inside her. Otherwise, we have our barracks at the command, seems to be quite a setup.

I get all of my things for the barracks, sign in and get ready to head out for the rest of the day. My hand is starting to not hurt, but have strange feelings, a sort of buzzing. I'm not all that concerned about it though. I get into the ships Radio Shack. There are only four or five regular Radioman, so we have to keep watch on each other. Not in a security way, but into requesting time off or leave or anything like that. With my rate, I am a Third-Class Petty Officer, going for my Second-Class promotion. The chief overseeing Communications seems quite impressed with my record. The one Petty Officer above me is Second Class getting ready for his First-Class promotion. Just so everyone knows, these promotions are not automatic. Not at all.

First off, you have to be recommended. After that, you have a test. Then, after all of that, you have to be chosen for your promotion, depending on your recommendation, test results, location in the world, how many on your command or ship going for the promotion in your field and then finally, your record.

I am not too worried going for my Second Class. My history is good, my training and schooling are very good and my personnel evals are very good, my average is three point eight. Out of four oh, not too bad!!

After being on board the mine sweep for a month or so, we have to head underway. I am not that crazy about it, obviously because of my getting sea sick, so I go to the corpsman on board and get some Dramamine. It works great for me! No seasick, no queasy feelings and no being tired. The chief and everyone are happy about that! The chief gets so happy that he, remembering my records, sets up a Morse Code drill. You see, I am the only Code operator onboard.

So now, we get everything set up and ready. My hand is hurting a bit but is doing OK; the index finger was the one with the most damage. It would not bend at the knuckle, so it appears to be an extra "something" sticking out there. But, again, all is cool. The send, encode, is done with the wrist and the fingers making short dit's and dashes. The receiving, or decoding, is done on a manual typewriter, just like in school. In order to graduate class, we had to send eighteen and receive twenty-two words a minute. So, here I am, in a radio shake, underway, with these headphones on my head, these ear pieces covering my ears and the chief and a few others hanging over the back of me watching what I am doing! No pressure though!! Finally, we get through with all and we pull into port. The chief, Executive Officer and some others go through the results of the whole crew. I find out later on that everyone was happy with the code. However, we had been having some other technical problems too though. It seems that over the past couple of weeks we have been having some communications problems.

After the Morse Code drill and all, the chief and I have a talk about the problem. You see, we have been having a problem transmitting. We discuss the problem and he allows me to get some tests done while in port. While these tests are being done to the ships, no one is allowed to be climbing their own ships ladders. So, I get the OK and the tests are done and I go for the results. Not good. I head over to the chief and explain all. Meanwhile, I go and collect all maintenance records on that particular. They are not adding up. According to the records, all is being done properly. So, the chief ask me what our options are. I explain to him that the problem seems to be a bad connection between the antenna itself and the receiver. I explain the only way to find out and make sure is to remove this thirty-foot-high steel antenna from its base and see what is happening. He trusts me because, again. I have gone through Antenna Maintenance School.

So, we rent a crane. We hook it up to the crane and she starts to pull. We have to be very careful though because it may be adhered to the base. After a while of trying, she comes loose, and water comes pouring out of it. Because, upon viewing the maintenance forms, lifting the antenna and water pouring out, the chief decides to put the Leading Petty Officer up for Captains Mast. Not Court Martial, but a discipline hearing in which he gets knocked down two rates. But then, I am made Leading Petty Officer!

I am going through all and the pain in my hand is getting worse every few weeks. I finally decide to go and have it checked out. The doctor looks at it and asks me why I still have it attached. I explained that it was my decision. At the time there was no pain or anything like that. Granted, I had no movement from the middle of the finger and it was, well, a pretty shade of blue due to the lack of circulation!! LOLOL. So, we discuss options.

We have decided to remove the top half of the finger. It was, in a weird way, in the way. I had no feelings in the top half, little blood flow and little movement. It was more in the way then out. Eventually, it gets done.

Although it may seem like a big thing to some folks, too me, it is just like, well, a walk in the park. Yes, it is my right hand, my dominant one, but at least now, there is no pain and no discomfort. Plus, now there is not something in the way. Remember, I had only some pain in the nub along with no movement. The finger was always sticking out so I could not even make a fist.

After all is done, my doctor now states that he will start the paperwork on my medical discharge. "SAY WHAT??" This was not even a single thought in my mind, nor a part of any conversation in any doctor's! Not this one, nor any others!

When I asked him where this decision came from, he just asked, "Well, you are a Radioman, right?" I replied "Yes" he then explained "That, well, your finger is off so you will have less use of your hand, and this is my direction." Then I asked him for a typewriter so I can show him that I can still properly function in my position. He replied, "Well, I don't have time for all of that. If you want to fight it later on, go ahead." I left his office with my head going, well, nuts. I had some major thoughts going on then.

The timing was not so good. It is now December. My enlistment is up in February. I could take the twenty per cent disability discharge, or I could fight it and win for what? If I won, I would be eligible to re-enlist, with a bad feeling with the way some people, like doctors, can misuse their position. I could fight and lose and still be medically discharged and just have wasted time, or I could take the medical discharge and get increasingly paid monthly as tax free money. Well, while I am thinking about it, remember my buddy Dan? He and I and another friend of ours, Paul, talk ad discuss my options. It is not a very long decision, obviously, but a final one. I take the discharge. Now, though, I have an option: take five thousand dollars as a lump sum now and wait for my monthly payment of one hundred and fifty dollars from them monthly ads up to five thousand dollars. So, I've decided on taking the five thousand dollars.

Well, let's just say that man that was a great decision! I am only given five days' notice of my discharge! So now, here I am living in Newport RI, being given five days' notice of no job, no house, and no way to get around town, no car and no license! Oh man! Talk about a dilemma! So, I start to talk with another new friend, David. He works on the base, also in the Navy, at SIMA. Shore Intermediate Maintenance Activity. He is one of the guys that I met while trying to work on and fix the antenna on board my ship. A cool guy with a neat girlfriend, a neat gal that lives off base, obviously. I've only met her once or twice, but she is neat.

I finally get called from the personnel folks onboard the ship. They hand me my discharge papers and now I am a Free Man!! What an interesting date of departure: Christmas Eve, 1984!!!

Chapter 10

Well, now I am an actual former "squid", as some folks call us. I am out of the Navy, and now need a job and a place to hang my hat. The place I choose to hang, until something else comes along, is The Newport YMCA. My buddy Dave and I head over there so I can get myself in there and get my room and get changed and we can head out for a party! He gives me a hand and then leaves so he can get to his girl, Phyllis, and then we can head out to our favorite bar, Jeremiah's. He gets back without her so the two of us head out. Man, I am so happy that she is not there. I say it only because it's a guy's time to hang out, drink lots, look at and dance with the girls out there and then hit Howard Johnson's for breakfast at around two am.

I am out of the Navy for about two days. I am already starting to worry about not having a job. So, I pick up a newspaper and start going through the ads for "Help Wanted". I go through them and I also start walking around town. I have been in town for around six months or so. I have seen the convenience stores and the hotels. The parking lots and the bars. So many things that I can do, but one thing that no one has: communications. So, I start applying in person. The first job that I got was as a uniformed security guard.

Remember, this was all before this thing called internet. As well as security guards getting some kind of respect. As a uniformed security guard, you were just a somebody/ nobody that just walked around and had no actual qualifications as a regular person. Well, I am just glad that I had a job. One of the good sides is working at night. That left me open for a regular job during the day. While doing the job thing at night, I also know that I need a better income. I remember the hotels in the town as well as the bars. The bars are out. Hey, here I am, flew around the world in the Navy, spent time in Sicily and Italy and Spain. On boards a ship going to Europe, visiting Finland, Denmark and England, having a TOP SECRET security clearance, seeing information from the CIA. But I cannot serve liquor, because I am twenty years old.

When my buddy David and I would go to Jeremiah's, we would have to get there before seven thirty. They started carding at eight. He and I use to have some memorable times there! They had liquor there that they made for themselves: Jeremiah's Weed! Oh man!! Enough about that part! So, we would start at seven thirty and go till closing. Then, he and I were heading out for breakfast. All eight of us or so! Now, I do not know if they finally realized that I was not twenty-one, but still.

So, I had to find an additional job. I knew with what I am making I could not afford a place as yet, so I needed to look quickly. I had to have some thoughts in mind though. First off, it had to be fairly close to my job now. Secondly, it had to be, not only where I am living now, but where I am looking for an apartment. And lastly, I did not have a car to go from place to place. Heck, I did not even have a driver's license! Heck, who needs a license to drive a boat!! LOLOL.

I have stopped in at a Real Estate office to look for a place. I speak with the gal at the office and then tell her that I am going for a second job. I leave there and head for a second job, the HOTEL VIKING. Not the Viking Hotel, mind you! I head inside and ask for an application. They've asked me for what position. I tell them that I will work any position, Front Desk, Security or even Maintenance. They hand me the form and I start to fill it out. When I get done I'm told that someone will get back to me, but as I am almost at the front door heading out, an older and shorter gentleman yells for me. I stop and turn around. Turns out that this is the owner, Dr Cohen. Man, am I impressed! If anyone here today reading this, I hope lots and lots and lots, ever has a chance to visit Newport, GO!!!!!!!! Anyway, he and I start talking and he asks when I can start! I tell him that I do have one job, midnights, and would have to see about moving hours around and all. He sighs though. You see, he wants me to work midnights till eight. I quickly run numbers through my head. The hotel is going to start me at a dollar more an hour plus benefits after three months. I have to consider the hotel, the security job, the YMCA, my place to live. Remember that by now, I have been out of the Navy only about a week or so, so I have been a very busy guy doing and thinking about a lot of options.

Remembering that I have the five thousand dollars in my pocket, burning away while I go job hunting and apartment looking, I agree to the Dr Cohen's offer for the job. I know that I have only worked for them for only a short while, but still.

So I call the security folks about their job and uniform, then I contact real estate gal. She answers the phone and we start talking and she has an apart for me to see. It is a single bedroom, furnished, not far from the hotel. She and I go to meet at Parker Avenue the next day. After hanging up, I get in touch with David and let him know what is going on. He decides to meet me at the apartment today. So, he and I meet and decide that it seems like a cool place, all finished and one bedroom for three hundred? All utilities included? He and I both think that it is a great deal. Plus, there is off street parking. Well, as I tell David, "I'm not too worried about that. Heck, I don't even have a license! Let alone a car!" He starts to laugh and says, "Well, we can change that."

The next day, I get shown the apartment. Obviously, I take it and get the key and sign the lease. David meets me there and we head to YMCA to get my stuff. That part seems to have gone real well! Between the job switch and the apartment. So now, Dave, I guess, wants to keep the good luck rolling, so we discuss the driving thing.

We have decided that I need a car, or as I told him, a license first. He figures that, if I get the car first, the license has GOT to come by real quick! So we start looking around at cars. I see one that I really like. A 19 81 blue Toyota Corolla. We head up to see a salesman and I decide I like it and want it. So, we head in for the paperwork and sales and everything. All looks good at first, but then they run into a problem. They like the Navy part, but not too happy with my job stuff. The only way that they will sell me the car is if I get a cosigner. So, David signs, but first tells me, "I know you won't make me may for this! I know where you live!!" The salesman and I laugh and hands me the keys. David takes them and away we go!!

The next day or so, I now head out for a job at the convenience store, Store 24. I go and apply for it and get told to come back in two days. I head back early on the second day and all seems good here. I have now taken Store 24 and Hotel Viking. Is not so bad. The manager here, I guess, is OK with how things are going. Occasionally I have to play like a rabbit and switch my times and days off between all, but still. Finally he takes me to the side and informs me that I am eligible for a promotion. He wants to make me Assistant Manager. With a nice raise and stock options and then the ability to transfer to another store should I want to? That is, once I get Manager. We talk about it. He, at the last minute, informs me that, "Oh yeah. As assistant, you have to come in whenever the new relief does not show up!" I tell him "No thanks." Understand, this is Newport. The folks that are hired are only part-time folks. So it is very easy for someone to just not show up. Plus, I tell him that this is again, only part time for me also. Along with the others. The difference is that I do always show up. Granted, I hadn't run into those problems, but I did not want to get involved with it either!

So now, let me see if I can remember all now, so far as the jobs and the car and the apartment. I have the job at Hotel Viking. I am just doing security stuff. By security stuff, I mean that I am walking around helping guests, checking vacant rooms to make sure no one is "borrowing" any for a day or a night or for a few hours.

The hotel is actually a good enough size. There are five stories in the hotel itself, plus an occasional open roof for special parties or viewings, like the July4th fireworks. There is an additional motel added to it. That is, motel floors that have been added twice. The location is fantastic also. You can stay at the hotel, keep your car parked there and take a walk to downtown, Thames St. With The Hotel being on Bellevue Ave, heck, it is right down the street from all of the mansions! I know that this may seem like a plug for the hotel, but it's not. I love Newport that much and cannot speak highly enough for it!

I have been working two jobs and things are going pretty well. You see, my foster mother has brought up, not only her own children, but us foster also. I guess the best way that I can put it is something I have taught both of my sons: If it is moral, ethical and legal, there should be nothing stopping you!

While working, I always kept my eye on the newspaper and help wanted ads.

Remember when I first got stationed in Newport, I am on the USS EXPLOIT, and I told you about SIMA with David and all? Well, there was another command there: Naval War College. It is a school for officers for certain priorities. Not just war games at NWC, but another being called SWOS Surface Warfare Officer School. Well, there was one other system I liked there. No, it was not a war game school. You see, because the base has so many commands in there, there has to be a way to communicate.

Well, that is where I come in. NTCC NEWPORT RI. Naval Telecommunications Communications Center. The handled communications and messages for the whole command, along with any guests along the way. But things were tough for them now. You see, I had my clearance and all. Remember that I was discharged one year ago? Well, if the clearance was not used for one year, it is pulled and put in as "HOLD" or ineffective or invalid. So they had to rush and run to get everything done before my time came up! Today is the last day of November!

OK. Now all is set and now, well, I have three jobs! A full-time at NTCC Newport, a full-time at the Hotel Viking and a part time at Store 24. Plus, remember that I still have those friends of mine, Dan, Paul and David. Between jobs after job after job, let us just say that I have no real time for life. I decide that I have to make some changes in my life. I have decided that I need to cut some job off. When my alarm clock goes off and I need to take ten minutes sitting on my bed trying to figure out the time, the day and which shirt I need to put on. That time has come. Plus, well, to be honest, because there is someone else.

I have met this girl at the Viking. Or rather, she has met me. I work security and she works at the front desk. There is a "rule" about employees dating each other. We meet and talk while at work. And, I will say that she is VERY VERY easy on the eyes. I have not been out of the Navy for too long, just over a year now. I know that it may seem like plenty of time to some, but I am just barely starting to live the "free life", so I am just trying to take it slow. We have only been working together a month or so, but Kristi starts saying certain somethings. Nothing real big or anything like that, just some small things sometimes connected with a wink, or a certain comment. She has done this several times and, well, I just try to ignore the comments. Well, let's just say that I did four times! Then I finally decided to take on the challenge! Boy, was I glad I did!

We decided that we both get along very well, like two peas in a pod, as some say. You see, though, there is that dating rule about employees. We think we have a way around it though. She is at the desk and I am doing my security rounds everywhere else. So we are never together. Problem solved. We try to keep some distance between us, but with the managers there, knowing about us, they are actually OK and try to set our hours together. Not too bad, eh? After not too long, though, she sees all of the hours that I am working.

The amount of work that I am doing and agrees that I need to do something about it. So I decide to quit Store 24 and make the Viking part time. This will keep me full-time at NTCC with my part being OK. There is one problem though. You see, the government job is changing shifts. Boy is this fun or what?? The hotel is fine with this as long as the two other part timers are OK with filling in. So now I am OK with my hours and, well, so is she.

Unfortunately, I do not get to hang with Dan and Paul as much as I would like to. Granted, we are known as The Three Amigos. No, we were not going out and getting drunk and acting like nuts. We were just three guys that hung around together. Whether it was Dan and Paul's place in downtown Newport, my apartment, or any of the many restaurants or Paul's family, who lived and grew up in town, we do get to hang. OK. Confession time. You see, again, Dan is starting as a professional male model. So, he obviously very good looking. So whenever we all went out with Dan, we got the second hand leftovers! You know, the ones that Dan denied, we, his buddies, get the second take!

Paul has been starting the job thing. He has been starting a career as a plumber. Granted, he is only twenty years old, he has been doing this for a few years. He has been working for a local guy or two, but he seems to be doing really well with it!

David and his girl got along with me and my gal. Once a week or two the four of us, along with anywhere from one to three other couples would get together at his girlfriend's apartment and we would smoke our cigarettes, cigars or pipes and play cards. You know the games. Jacks To Open and Trips To Win, etc. granted, I was never real good at cards, but what the heck, we all had a blast!

Time continued and we all, even to this day, stayed close, The Three Amigos, and David. Life continued and my lease was coming up for renewal. My girl and I have decided to move in together, but not here. We were looking for another place. She was on month to month and my lease expired so we got rid of our old places and found a new one, Middletown RI. Next town from Newport. She has also found another job at a closer place to the new apartment. Doing the same job, just for a brand new inn, privately owned by two brothers. Nice small place right across the street from a large grocery store. Things seem to be going very well between us. With my full-time job at NTCC and part-time at the Viking and she working full-time at the hotel, bills are getting paid and life is not so bad.

While living in Newport, I find that I have some relatives living in town, as well as some living two towns over, Portsmouth. I come from a military background. Nothing like an overboard military one, but enough military to be proud of. My adopted dad was Navy. Granted, he was drafted to do his time as a Navy SEA BEE, as well as a fighter, in Vietnam. My uncle was a Radioman just like me, in the Navy. One grandfather was in the Army. We all are very happy and very proud of what we have done. There is more to us than just the Army and Navy thing. In Portsmouth, RI I have a great Uncle and Aunt. He was a professional chef in the Navy. He worked at the White House under Eisenhower. He was the head chef there! And I will say that he was a FANTASTIC chef even after and during retirement and then some. My great aunt and uncle lived in town with one of their daughters and her two kids living in Newport.

One of his hobbies on the side was shooting. There was a private place in town that was owned by some other former military guys there. On certain weekends they would go up into their clubhouse with families, bring up their barbeque meat, not just ANY meat. If one of the guys went out hunting, we would roast up deer meat. The hamburger meat was not just from-the-grocery store meat. Again, all was fresh meat. While grilling the meat, some of the guys would bring their own guns too. They would have the shooter yell "PULL" and a clay piece would be released into the air and the guy, or gal, would have to shoot it out of the   sky! Iam no fantastic sharp shooter, but I did OK. With the number, and ages, of the guys there, I did get to do some other shooting. Not just with a rifle, but I did get to shoot an Uzi, Glock 9mm and a 45. target practice was always fun, but remember, never at any time did anyone forget about the guns, the bullets and the safety. Everyone kept in touch with knowing how many and where the kids were, where and how many bullets were there and what could happen IF someone messed up.

Again, life is going very well. I think that if there was really something like a before life, I must have been a fish or a whale or something like that. I just cannot get away from the water! Between Newport, Norfolk, San Diego and Maryland! I cannot or will not leave the ocean! Whether it is first ting in the morning, last thing at night or anywhere in the middle! Kristi and I are out for a nice ride. Out near Cliff walk. We are driving in the car enjoying the weather, nice and warm, no clouds, and the sound of the ocean with her turning swills. We are driving and all seems to be going well for my surprise.

I pull over to a parking lot facing the water. Remember when I said earlier about our minds thinking alike? Well, tonight was no exception. While listening to the radio, she just softly asks, "So, what do we do now? Where does life go?" I just simply ask her, "So now, what are you doing for the next sixty or seventy years?"

We are only engaged about six weeks. All continues going well with one quick bump. Nothing real big in any sense except that her father will not see his daughter living with a man until she is married. In a way, thinking back now, this may be just one small reason to push things along. She is not from Rhode Island, but from Connecticut. Only about a two and a half hour drive.

The family and I meet and we all get together very well. As far as my family is concerned, my adopted parents are introduced as my parents. Granted, my girl knows all about my adoption and brothers and foster family, but it is my decision to keep all things easy. A total number of brothers and sisters come to about eight brothers, three sisters, three mothers and one father! Man, talk about a Christmas list! No, seriously though, nothing like that at all from here. She has heard me talk of my brothers and sisters, but has only met some of them once or twice.

Anyway, things continue going on very well. I am not the kind of guy that just sits around day to day. I hope that everyone can see that part of me. Eventually, you will see just about that part of me goes. Not only for me, but my family too, including my kids. She and I move several times for better jobs, not for us, but for me. Well, maybe not for me, but for us. Every job that I/we have moved to have always been for an increase in either pay or job security. The one problem that did happen was when we moved out of state for a position with a phone company in New Jersey. We did move there from Connecticut for a more secure and better paying job, but while going through some physical training, I am laid off! Man was I scared! She did help me get through it though.

I went through the newspapers looking for a job. About four days later, after my fifth or sixth attempt, I am hired on the spot. I am working at a waterbed factory. Not an easy position. I am not a sales person or anything like that at all. This is the company warehouse. The company has about five offices in New Jersey. This is their corporate warehouse. So, depending on which office needs what, we are the guys that pull the beds, still in parts, the dressers and whatever else is ordered, like the night stands and whatever else. We have two lifters that we drive around to get pieces onto the fifth or sixth levels up...or down. The bosses there seem to be impressed with me working there. I usually try to get in fifteen minutes early and the last one to leave. Again, the bosses are impressed and sit me down in the office. They ask me how I feel about the job and all, including hours and money. Like any red blooded American, I would not mind a few dollars more. They laugh and tell me that there may be an option there for me. They are so impressed, they tell me that they want to make a non-existent position for me. Supervisor. There is no supervisor there. Just the boss in the office and us run arounds.

Honestly, I am quite impressed, well and happy. However, I tell them that I have to decline. I try this "Honesty" thing with them. I am telling them that I am very happy with the position that I am in and am pleasantly shocked that I would be requested for this position. However, as I explain, that I do not plan on making this company as "life term". I am happy with what I am doing now, however I am waiting to hear about another position with another company. I do not tell them the name because I do not want to jinx it, but between you and I, it's Xerox! So, back to work I go! No one upset and no one upset, and, unfortunately, no one a bit richer at the end of the week!(Now, I want everyone of you reading this to know that my then-wife is/was not a slouch at all! She has always been behind me when I needed to make a decision! Whenever we moved, yes, I got a job. Be it known though, so did she. To be totally open and honest, I am not sure if she is or has read this part, but I still do, and will, love her forever! After our divorce, I found someone else, but that did not work out. However, she has also. I can only wish her the best. I mean, yes, I still love her, partially because we have the two best boys in the world!! OK, now, back to the job thing...)

Work is going well for the both of us. She has a position as a bank teller, as her usual job. Whenever we have moved, she has always stuck with banking, plus, well it has stuck well with her too.

After working at the warehouse for about for months or so, I get a call from Xerox! You see, I have a brother- in-law that has worked there for quite a while. No, he cannot, as I had told him, not to get me a job there. About the one thing that he did do, though, is find out about openings and let me know where there were any. I asked him to not tell anyone anything about me. He never has. He just told me about several openings in my area, Connecticut and White Plains New York, as a technician, fixing the machines in customer's offices.

I get my call and go in for my interview in White Plains New York. As most people are, I am a bit afraid/ scared going for a job interview for a company like this! Here this is, a Fortune 500 company that most folks would give their left arm for!

It turns out that I am about to have a very full and busy day! I walk into the office and see about fifteen other guys, but no gals, trying for this position. In a way I am a bit afraid. I mean, there is nothing special about me at all, compared to all of these others. Here I am, a fairly freshly married twenty four or twenty five year old high school dropout, US Navy background with a medical discharge that has always worked at whatever was available.

The interview was interesting. It was actually a technological test had to take a math quiz first, then electronics, then spelling then just overall miscellaneous test. I guess I did pretty well. I mean, I passed all of those tests, which I am a bit scared of taking. I mean, I am not a stupid, yet I am not Einstein either! So after a while of taking all of these tests, I go for my interview. I head on in to see John.

We speak for a while as a regular interview but just seems like a bit long. A while later I finally learn why. He has to take some time while my results were graded. I guess I did OK because I was hired on the spot! I am both psyched and scared. Here my gal and I are in New Jersey in an apartment from Hell! Our neighbors downstairs in a two-family house do not, well, seem to get along too well. (The understatement of the year!) They have sole access to the basement which means that they have access to the circuit breakers. Yup, you got it! Whenever they have an argument or disagreement with us, off go one, or more, breakers.

My new job could not have come at a better time! We broke our lease, granted, due to us leaving early. Even though the landlady knew of the situation, we never got anything back. So we pack up all and get ready to head out to Connecticut. My girl talks with her mother and father and she and I agree with them to move into their house for a few months so we can save some cash. Her folks do not have a huge house, not at all. Just a regular one family place. They have a partially finished basement which makes that our bedroom/our place. Now we have been living there about six months. For a sort of "rent" or payment, I do the grass and snow and whatever else is needed.

My job with Xerox, again, is a technician. I would be working on the mid-size copiers. Not the small little desktop ones, but a bit larger one. The large enough size that they would easily make thirty thousand copies. Again, way before internet and computers. I am sure that you will remember the ladies, or gentlemen, sitting at their desks, typing something out on a type writer using twenty pound paper, pulling the page out, walking down the hall, putting the paper on top of this clear glass, punching in "20", then start, then bringing that to your desk, slotting one copy to each individual and then getting back to work!

In the mid-size copier sizes, there were about six or eight machines, variations of those sizes. Meaning that there could be one XEROX 1040, but there would be variations of the machine. One machine could have an automatic stapler, where, sitting right next to it, would be the same machine, but this one with an RDH, Recirculating Document Handler, something that would handle your originals.

I am the first tech on my team of about 12 that was trained on ever style of every mid-size machine that was in use in this part of the United States. To be honest though, I am not the best tech on the team. There were others there.

After school/training, I received my own assignment. Being that my team handled mid-volume machines in lower Fairfield County, my area was a part of Stamford. We were all given a vehicle to drive around in. I had a station wagon. We were each given a vehicle because, I guess, to make sure we had a way of getting around fairly easy. Well, plus with the amount of spare parts that we had to lug around with us! We were actually carrying around, I heard, anywhere from five to seventy-five thousand dollars each, depending on the style, type and amount of parts!

After the training, team placing and location of our individual assignments, Kristi and I decide that we have enough saved for our own apartment. We are both aware of that old saying, "It's not what you know, but who you know." A friend that knew we were looking for a place, said that she had a friend and her husband moving out of a two-family house in Ansonia. Ansonia is a nice small town that is eight point two square miles and has about eight thousand residents, so we are told. So we look around town and both like it and, well, decide to talk to the landlady. We speak for about twenty minutes and she asks about us moving in. Obviously, we say "Yes" and a date is all set up.

We inquire about a lease and she replies, "I do not want a lease. I figure that if I need one to protect me, then I have the wrong people living upstairs." That comment left us both on the floor, but hey, it works for us! The home owner turns out to be a very nice lady.

We move into this small town and decide to expand this thing called family life. We have only known each other about six months we are both aware of our likes and dislikes. We also know that we are both interested in the family life. That is, that we both want a family. Not a big family, maybe two or three kids. Granted now, we both love kids and want a family, but we both need to get to know each other more. You know, our likes and dislikes, plus just how we are going to be treating each other with and without the kids. No, we have no thoughts about the kids and numbers. Just how we are going to treat each other. We are just taking time with all.

My wife and I live upstairs and the landlady is downstairs. Along with the house is a nice two car garage, attached under the house, one side for her and one side for us. Well, I have a little something that I am interested in doing on the side for the heck of it. I like refinishing dressers and anything wood. A buddy of mine knows this and asks if I would mind refinishing an old dresser for him. I tell him that I would actually like doing it, but under a couple of conditions: 1) he buys the material 2) do not constantly bug me about it and 3) remember that I will let him know when it is done. No problems! So, Rich gets everything in about two weeks and drops the dresser off. Oh my god! Do I have my work cut out for me!

It turns out that the dresser once belonged to his grandmother and was laying in the attic for quite a while. That is, until his wife and she brought it downstairs and used it in his daughter's room where about anything and everything had been spilled on it!

So I start my work for a while. Like I said before, I like refinishing and, well, if I may say, am pretty darned good at it. I can tell because, after about a month or so of working on it, Rich picks it up and goes nuts over it. So nuts that, a couple of months later, he informs me that he sells it for five hundred dollars! Man, in a way, I am happy for him, but in another way, man am I pissed!!! lolol!!

While at home one day, I am taking a look at the newspaper. I see an article about an organization in town looking for volunteers. Like many towns, there is the normal Volunteer Fire Department, but there is also a volunteer ambulance and rescue organization, ARMS. Ansonia Rescue Medical Services. These are the folks that do the ambulance and rescue. In this town, the fire department just does fires. ARMS does everything else!

I know first-aid from cub scouts, that is about my extent of medical training, but I would like to find out more, so I head down to their organization to find out more. Well, come to find out that, like the fire department, these guys, and gals, are not paid. The go out and run for an ambulance call whenever. Now, please understand that Ansonia is a small town, only six point two square miles big, but the ambulance

My wife and I do make one large agreement though. Now, understand that we have no problems with babysitters, family or not, as well as having their grandma and grandpa, as well as aunts, uncles, brothers or sisters watching our child or children. But we have decided to try to watch our kids on our own, eventually. I go to work each day, and night when necessary, and she handles the kids.

We eventually have our two boys. Both planned and timed. The oldest, Craig, is born four years later. Todd was four years after him. Both normal and healthy and no problems. Both planned.

We have our family, the four boys and us. All is going well, except that we start having some problems. You see, I do not mind working more and more, as well as volunteering EMS in my town. She and I agree, remember, that I do the working, money stuff, and she takes care of the kids. No, I am not Ralph Kramden. Understand that I love my boys, and wife, more than anyone can imagine. Whenever I can, I take care of the boys. Like changing diapers etc. my wife, however, lets me go out on ambulance calls.

We appear, to us and to others, to be a very matched and loving couple. Well, we are. For now.

Well now, I guess that you will find out just why this book is being written. Not because I think that my life is so great and so wonderful that I should share it with the world, no. It is, basically to my therapist/ psychologist. I am being told that when I am not feeling too well, mentally or emotionally, to not keep it in. I was told the best thing was to start writing it all out. Well, so, here I, or rather, we go!

Well, remember a little while ago, I was telling you about my wife and I having problems? Well, I decided to make a major change. I decided that I need to spend more time at home and with the family.

Chapter 11

I eventually have taken a transfer with Xerox into New York City. I work in the offices. Not fixing the machines, but just internally in the offices for the City. I have been doing the job there for about five years. Putting the other position there, repair, I have been there for eight years. While there, I have, like so any other folks, decide to start my own business, Computer Security. No, the the program stuff!

You see, we are having a problem with people physically stealing computers from our floors! The Office Manager and I have a talk or two. He is aware of my background, TOP SECRET security clearances plus the Private Investigators training that I have had. The PI is not a very big deal, but hey, it impresses him. He wants to, I guess, try me first. You see, he tells me, that the thefts of the computers off of cubicles is not the only problem. It seems that someone has broken into his office several times. He is, so he tells me, is at his wits end. He has not reported his situation to the New York City sales manager or anyone else. He just wants me to come up with an idea to fix it...FAST!

He and I are in his office, so I ask him if there are any restrictions. "No way" he says. So I have an idea: take a wireless camera disguised as a smoke detector, or rather ALSO smoke detector, attach it to his ceiling, aim it toward his front door and have the signal transmitted to a receiver in a different office. This way, even if somehow someone figures out something, they will not be able to change anything. They will not know where the receiver is. I will set the recorder on a one and one half second recording to limit the recording time.

He has asked about the possible changes. In a way, I left Xerox. That is, I left the Corporation. Instead I decided to take a sales job selling Xerox office equipment. I found a company that needed help in sales, an independent company. My new office was only about a 20-25 minute drive. So now I obviously had more time to spend with my best parts.

Now, understand, some people think that I can sell snow to a snowman. Well, not really. I do OK. That is, well enough to get by! I know Xerox very very well. Between servicing the equipment in companies' offices to handling some of the Customer Service and Billing inquiries and Customer Upgrade inquiries, the company is quite happy to have me on their books. Plus, well, so am I. Not only to be working for a company in a new position for me, but mostly for the time to hopefully get the family back together.

AND A NEW ME HAS BEGUN

Chapter 12

My new job locally in a local town is not bad. Not a far drive, only about twenty-five minutes each way. I almost feel bad that I am not working or commuting like I was before.

The sales position to me is a bit new, that's for sure! So, I need to go in a little bit early to do some extra reading on Xerox's "responsibilities" as the actual owner and leaser of equipment to a separate company. But there is still one thing going on about me. I am still a "workaholic" it seems. I still am getting up early. OK, maybe not as early as I was while working in New York City, but early. That is, early enough to get up, get my paperwork together and be the first in my office to overlook my new sales area and see who might need what.

One thing I do want everyone to know right off the top: I love my wife and I love my kids more than anything I could ever dream about. I enjoyed working in New York. I enjoyed not only the folks that I worked with, but with any/all of the XEROX customers and clients that I met while down there. But I am a big boy and am very much aware of my situation and know and acknowledge the fact that I do need to change. Plus, well, if I am feeling this way about me, my wife, hopefully is aware of why I want to need to make these changes.

I am going into work to learn and do more with XEROX rules and responsibilities. My manager seems to be happy and impressed with the learning and accepting my new role. Actually, I have only been here about two or three weeks and he wants me to hit the floor running.

We go to one or two clients and he plays "Mr. Quiet" in the background.

Well, it is my first visit. No, I did not sell anything THIS time because he did not want me to. I am a bit confused. I mean, this is a sales job, no? Yup, it is but he just does not want me to sell because he wants to see how I react to customer's questions, etc.

We head out after the visit and start talking. Well, he is happy with the way that I have answered the questions and was happy that I did not promise the world to the customer. So off we go and now back to the office. Well, my FINAL DAY at the office!!

It is 1 7 August, 1997 and I am getting ready for work. One thing that I have done in the past several years being in New York City, is that I have learned to like my coffee a whole lot. I do me a WHOLE LOT!! I used to hate coffee, but no more. I need it to start my day, like so many others in life.

I have just gotten dressed, grabbed my coffee from the kitchen and am grabbing my keys to the car/ I get in, the car starts and all is running well. I happen to know how to drive and handle a car pretty well. I mean, heck, I went to school and learned how to drive an Ambulance for Ansonia! I have also double learned about respecting the road.

To give a quick view, Ansonia is in area called "The Valley" just because we are just like that. In order to get out of the area and into "regular town", like Orange or New Haven, we have to travel up and down some hills.

There is one back road that I take to get to New Haven that has a lot of turns as well as hills. The road is usually very quiet because of the turns which is why I like it so much. It is also a road that, although has signs for 3 5 and 40MPH, I usually take it a bit slower. Again, I call it a respect for the road. A nice quiet turning road. That is all I remember.

You see, my wife gets a visit from Ansonia Police Department. It seems that my car has been in a single-vehicle accident. Car hits Tree. The police ask her if she would like to have an officer stay while she contacts someone to watch them. She declines and gets a hold of someone quickly.

She goes to Yale New Haven Hospital to see what is going on. She gets there and she is told some bad news. Seems that I am not expected to make it. While in a coma for two and a half weeks my heart stops twice and I have to be defibbed! Meanwhile, she contacts some friends so they know what is going on. Some friends try to contact me because we have not seen each other in a while.

For example, remember my friends Paul and Dan? Well. Paul called my house to see how all is going. We have not spoken in a while and he just wants to say "HI". So, he calls the house. My wife answers. Paul asks for me and she explains that I am in the hospital and not expected to make it. Paul is in shock so he calls Dan and lets him know what is happening. Dan decides to drive up from Pennsylvania and Paul down from New York State.

Now, let me explain something to you: I was not wearing a seat belt. So, my chin went forward and dented the steering wheel. Then, I bounced back so hard that I broke the driver's seat and was found later laying on the back seat! If I were wearing one, the most damage would have been to my left leg and heel. Upon impact, the ankle was squeezed between the metal frame and the seat slider. The car was pushed that close together.

I have just spent two and a half weeks in a coma. Was visited by family and friends, my heart had to be restarted twice, and I have no memory of any of this. I have no memory from the morning of the accident, 1 7 August 199 7 until almost Christmas that year.

CHAPTER 13

I am just starting to wake up. Not quite sure what I am seeing or feeling. Things seem sort of strange to me. I am here in some bed, laying on my back looking at the ceiling.

But some things just feel so strange to me. I go to move my head to see what is next to me. But I cannot! My head just will not turn. Not to the left and not to the right. Not up and not down. Not at all. So now I try to move my arm. It too is stuck. ALL parts of me are stuck! I cannot move ANY part of my body at all! I am TOTALLY paralyzed!!!

Eventually, a nurse comes by, I think. That is to say that I do remember that I am first realizing that I am paralyzed. I just do not remember any conversations with anyone.

The paralysis is from head to toe. Well, that is....except my eyes. I have to blink them, "Once for 'yes' and twice for 'no'".

I am not sure if I am afraid, scared, mad or sorry for myself. I am the kind of person that is happy to help others. To do things for someone or anyone else. Whether they need it or not. I am not one of those proud guys. I will ask for help when I need it. Granted, maybe when I have gotten to so far a point that I can almost never get back/ But still. I am not over the cliff, just to the end of it.

While I am laying there, I see a couple of things with my boys. Not sure where, but my oldest, just 7 now, I seeing sitting on the floor with his legs crossed, his head being held up by his left hand, trying to make sense of whatever he is seeing. My 3-year-old is with his mom on a chair.

Just around Christmas time I realize that I am not in a hospital. I am at Gaylord Rehab in Woodbridge CT. The nurses are turning me from one side to the other to put a board under my back so they can slide me onto a rolling bed and bring me down to physical therapy. They are doing this twice a day.

My wife shows up there occasionally to help. The boys are coming by once or twice a week. My mom drives an hour and a half a couple of times, 3x times a week roughly, just to see me and take care of me too. Eventually, I see a mirror and I see why my little guy is so confused. He does not quite know who I am. Understandably, neither can I!

Due to the accident, because I did not have on my seat belt, my chin hits the steering wheel. So hard, my teeth, chin and jaw have to be worked on. They have my teeth wired shut and a chin brace going from ear to ear. Eventually, I am to find out it took two to three doctors almost eight hours!

Finally, the brace is removed and Todd sees me, raises his arms towards me, and runs to me smiling and yelling "Daddy!"

I realize that I have a choice every day: I could just lay there and feel sorry for myself or I could do something about my situation. Not only for me, but for my boys. I could teach them what it means and what you can do by fighting everything within yourself with yourself. In other words, don't just accept the situation, but to fight it and work on it and improve everything you can any way you can. I am soon to realize that this is not just a one-time decision to make. It is a constant decision. No, it is not a quick fix that will solve things right there and then. But a constant reminder that the decision is made BY me and FOR me. No one else can make that decision.

Remember when I said that my wife and I are having problems? Well, they do not just go away just because I am not at home. One day she asks me about a friend of mine. Or rather an acquaintance. He has come by to visit me with a "friend" of his. Two guys.

One day she asks me if I ever had sex with this guy. I honestly answer "Yes". It was not the question that I had expected, not the reply I had expected either. I never had a chance to explain that this guy had confronted me several time. I just tried to be the guy who declined. Not the guy who replied and ran. After several requests, I finally let my guard down and let him go oral on me. That was the extent of it. However, I was never given the chance to explain anything to her. I have just realized the LARGE error that I had made! No, we did not have the sex stuff. However, I did let him try SOMETHING on me.

Now, understand, I realize that it was not THAT moment that her decision was made. However, it was a MAJOR part of it. Things were never the same again.

She did, however, bring my boys once a week or so to see me at Gaylord. I was doing pretty well. I was using a walker for a bit to walk around. Otherwise, however, I was in a wheel chair. The accident did some nice, if you can call it that, damage to my spine. One vertebra in my neck and two in my mid-lower back.

The neck vertebrae has half my face and throat partially paralyzed, so I talk strange and swallow my food strange. The two in my back is why I need my chair.

While at physical therapy, again, my walking is doing better and the feeling to my arms are getting better, but the movement seems to be decreasing. All in all though, I do seem to be getting better overall and soon it is time to leave therapy. So now, off I go to Brookfield, CT. An outpatient group home for the handicapped.

The house itself is nice, so is the staff. The house is in a residential community, not fat from our physical therapy place or the mall. I have my own room. Just like a regular house with my regular bedroom. Regular TV and regular radio. Some of the other clients go to therapy too.

One client is a lad. A school teacher that was in a car accident. She is in an electric chair plus has some mental problems. There is an elderly man there too. He was injured in some kid of apartment fire or something like that. He, too, is in a chair. Then there is a third guy. A former firefighter. While on the roof of a house, the roof caved in and he ended up going down by the chimney. Physically he is OK, no chair required. But mentally he is having MAJOR problems. He brings himself into the bathroom and stays there for three or four hours. Then there is me.

After seeing these folks, I realize just how lucky I am. Yes, I have some physical problems as well as the mental one. But nothing at all like these folks!

Eventually I talk to the staff and I explain that, yes, I am here because of the accident and all, I cannot stay so long, so many hours in a day, with these other clients. I do need to get out more and do more with regular folks. A job or something!

After talking to whomever, I get the OK and work part time in the Danbury Mall at Sears. Selling computers, TV's and stereos! I guess I am doing OK in there because, well heck, I am there for a while! But I also think and realize that I really do not need the cash but some of the folks that I work with do. So, I speak with the customers and get whatever lined up for a purchase, I hand them over to another salesman. You see, we are paid ONLY by commission. No salary. Again, these folks need it more than I do. So, this just makes things a bit easier for them. Rather than fighting back and forth for whomever comes around to maybe buy something! My work at Sears continues for a while.

No, I am not considered as such a great seller, but I do OK.

After a few months there, I take a trip home for an overnight visit. The living room is made into a bedroom for me to sleep. I am HOPING for my wife and I to sleep together. No, not for the lovemaking and all. Just to see if maybe we could spend the night together like an average couple. No fighting and yelling. Just to be with one another. A friend of ours, Rich, comes over. So does a rep from my insurance company.

It is a good thing that this happened while going to see a client. The company I worked for is covering this as Workers Comp.

Their representative comes over with an architect. We are sitting down and looking at the possible changes and additions to be made to the house for me. We are all sitting there at the kitchen table. That is, except for my wife. She is up and doing other things in the kitchen, living room and the boys. She is seeming distant. That is, until the phone rings. Then almost all hell breaks loose!

As much as I would like to get into it, I won't. But let's just say that a pleasant time was not had by anyone that day. That is, except for my boys. One good thing about she and I is that we both agree that the boys always come first.

Anyway, while working in Danbury and living in the area, I go on some regular doctor appointments. For example, for my elbows. Or rather, a lack-thereof! (The lack of movement) I go to the Orthopedic to find out what is going on with why they are moving less and less and now almost not at all. I have about 5degree in my left elbow and none in my right. The orthopedic doctor takes some ex rays and reviews my records. We sit down and talk.

He explains that, due to the accident, I have extra bone growth. The growth is both elbows, one shoulder and both knees. Basically, my brain has had a hiccup. It is telling my body to just make bones...wherever it wants to! So I ask him "What do we do about it?" He explains that he will have to go in and reconstruct or redesign my elbows, knees and shoulder. I am sooooo happy now! I finally have a reason for all of this weird stuff going on with me!

So, I ask him, "When do we start?" He explains that we have to wait for six to nine months after the accident so my brain can calm down. The Traumatic Brain Injury could confuse the surgery and think it is another accident and re-start bone growth! So awaiting we will go!

After waiting a few more months, surgeries are started. Many people may not, but I remember that I am in control of my body and my situations. I decide which operation on whichever part of my body that I need. So I decide to do work on my left leg because the extra bone is getting in the way of my straightening it out. However my right leg, although not looking too wonderful, is, for the most part, just fine. I also go, obviously, for both of my elbows. The left shoulder though does not seem to be going through any problems so, if it is not broken, why fix it?

Each of the surgeries are independent from each other. So I go in three times. Thankfully, all is done and, with physical therapy, I can finally be a normal person again that is, well, as normal as one can get!!!

You may or may not believe how much a visit from family or friends can do to someone. Especially someone going through these kinds of things. I pluralize it because I am dealing with 1) paralysis 2) probable divorce 3) a whole new way of living my life.

One day I get a call from my foster family. Remember them? The three sisters and a brother from the family? My foster mom and the family come driving up from New Jersey to Connecticut. Granted this may not seem long, but one sister lives in Long Island and my foster mom is about seventy years old. A two to three hour trip is not easy for her. But regardless, she drove all this way to see me! The whole family has!

After a while, I get a visit from a friend. A very good friend from a while ago. Remember my friends from Newport RI? Well one day both Paul and Dan show up! I am almost out of breath! My two friends from what seems like an eternity ago, show up at my home! They are there for a while and we talk about anything and everything. It almost seems like we have never been separated!

The employees at the group home are some real great ladies and guys! They seem well able to handle about any situation that comes up with any of the clients. One day, though, I hear two or three of them arguing. No, not hard and rough and all. I guess you could call it a minor disagreement.

My buddies and I are in my room having lunch. Nothing fantastic and all, just some takeout from one of the local places. My buddies and I are listening a bit and start to laugh. You see, most of the staff there, twenty- four hour coverage, start doing some arguing about the schedule. It seems that ALL of them want to be working on whichever day my friend Dan, the made model friend, is coming to visit! In the meantime, Paul is always coming too! So either way, they want to find out when my friends are visiting so they would have a chance with my buds!!

Eventually during one of their visits, I have to take a ride somewhere. So I get brought onto one of those large van for the handicapped. After about a ten-minute ride or so, we stop by Candlewood Lake. I get brought down and see Paul there with his wife and family. Seems that they like the area a lot and bought a house by me. As Paul explained it, they both liked the house and the area. Then they actually put me into their decision! I was almost floored when they told me this! So now, on nice Saturdays or Sundays, the group home folks would drive me to Paul's' house to spend the day with him, his wife and kids. That is to say, when I was not work at Sears.

Hhmmmm...I guess you can say that, in a strange way, I am a lot like the rest of the WORKING world. Having friends, having a separate place to hang my hat and a job. Granted, not like the one I had in New York City, but hey, I got out occasionally!

Eventually, after three years though, it was time for me to go to a different place. No, not another group or hospital or anything like that. But to my own place. Well. Being that I was now divorced and her boyfriend was living in my house, what is next? My insurance company and I take a few trips from Brookfield CT to New Haven CT.

We had several certain things to require: Obviously it had to be handicapped accessible, handicapped equipment down to the bathroom and tub to counter height accessible as well as closet and cabinet accessible. The insurance people and I talk and looked around. I also asked them if I could get a 2 bedroom place. That way when my boys came over, there would be a place for them too. In a way, I could hardly believe it, but they agreed right off of the top! No begging and no pleading. Just "OK".

Eventually my move was made and I got into a very nice, only a ten year old, fairly new building.

Not too long from my move, I had my kids visiting me in my apartment. After the first visit or two, we stated to head outside and see the town a bit. We went to Dunkin' Donuts for a frosty thing for us.

There was an open are concert setup on the town green for consents and shows and all. There were also some folks walking dogs in the area. It looks like a pretty OK place.

After a few visits, as I was told by my boys, a message from my X's boyfriend, that if I wanted to continue seeing the boys, I would have to give their mom fifteen dollars per visit to pay for gas. This did not see as a discussion but rather an order. No Pay, No Play. So now, for the obvious reasons, I paid

After moving to my apartment things were doing OK. In one of my visits to Gaylord Rehab, I needed my regular motor-powered wheel chair. I was admitted because I needed surgery on my knee. The company that I used for repair to my chair was called. I asked to have them pickup my chair from the apartment and deliver it to me here.

When the young lady that handled the move brought it to me, I was very...uummm...pleased! She was an awfully attractive gal! She brought the chair to my room and we talked a bit. That is, well, we talked about the chair for ten minutes. We talked about anything else for two hours! I spent two or three weeks in rehab and this gal would come by each day, not to visit me. She had her own job, as well as her own daughter, about the same age as my oldest son. But, rather, to drop me off a cup of coffee. She knew how addicted I was to my morning caffeine trip! But she also knew too late in the day was not a good thing either. So, she would swing by, see if I were busy and, if I was, just drop off the coffee.

However, if I was free, we would sit and talk.' During the day, for about half an hour or so. But later on, we would sit and watch TV or talk.

Eventually I was discharged, and I moved back to my apartment. Eventually she moved in also along with her daughter. She had one half custody of her so she was not there all of the time. We, she and I as well as her little one and my boys got along well. Yes, there were some problems occasionally, but not often at all..

Things were moving at a much quicker phase then earlier while living in the group home! Me, my boys visiting, now my new girlfriend and her daughter. Well, now one more: A vehicle! I had just received a call from the insurance company and we talked about transportation. The brought up a handicapped mini-van.

My girl, like I said, moved in and all is going well. I am speaking with the insurance company about the van. I finally contact DMV. Coming to find out that I have to go through a special class for driving this mini-van. So now, the van is delivered and all is running well.

Remember when I mentioned about the gas thing for the boys? Well, my girlfriend and I have discussed it and she has agreed to bring the boys back from their weekend visits. Like I said, all five of us get along well so there is no problem with that. Thankfully though, I am saving about fifteen dollars every two weeks or so. Also, though, she is driving the boys back, but only until I get my license. After that, the drive is my responsibility.

The driving and learning has not been long. Nor was it too tough. I guess. The training took about a month or six weeks. Believe me, it was a bit different. I was used to using my legs and feet for increasing my speed or slowing down and breaking. But now, though, the handicap vehicles are made with a hand control. I push forward to break, but it pulls it down to speed up. Not too difficult, but if you have been driving for a while, it is a bit different. Well, no more paying for trips and all!

After a while, my girl and I talk a bit. She asks me how/why my divorce. She knows that I am not very comfortable talking about it so we have ignored the subject for a few months. But she inquiries about it. I am not a liar at all. I have not wanted to discuss the subject, so it had been some peace. However, now I tell her the situation of the one oral time with a guy.

Well, let's just say that it went over peacefully, but that was it! After a few weeks we could feel the tension in the apartment. The silence at bed time. The silence in the morning. So now, after about a two-to-three-week period, she is packing her things away and moving into a small apartment by her fathers.

I tell the boys at our next visit. When I pick them up. They are sad that I am sad, but they also know that NO ONE can take the place of their mother.

Things continue as normal, I guess you can say, as any other normal foes. My boys and I get along GREAT with each other! I hope that it has something to do with my helping to raise them. Even if it is for 2 full weekends a month and each Tuesday after school. Some things that they learn about me is that my YES means YES. Not by hollering or yelling, but by learning that if they re-ask, the answer will still be the same.

My youngest, now about ix or so, is having some problems with school. Not with fighting, but with school projects. I can see that he is trying very hard. Unfortunately thou, I can see his frustration. I get a call from my wife and she explains the situation with him and the request that she come in and talk with her. I tell her that I would like to be involved also. So the meeting comes with my ex-wife, her boyfriend/husband, the teacher and I. The teacher is very nice and explains the situation with us. With the frustration with his schoolwork. She then states that she is impressed to see me, my ex and her man. She is actually happy to see all of us involved. As I explain it, "Well, all three of us will have to handle the situation on a whole. No part-time help at home and nothing with him being with me".

We talk for a while and get things put in place so we are all rowing the same boat. After we leave we all discuss the meeting in the school parking lot.

Several days later, I call my sons mom on the phone. I explain that I have been doing some research and discussing my little guys' situation. I find out about some testing being done at Yale Children s Study. We all agree to take my son and get him tested and find out if there is anything we should know about, as well as any hints.

My youngest son has several visits to do there. After all is said and done, it appears that he has a small piece of ADHD. Nothing very large. No enough for any medication or anything like that. Just a bit on the slow side. The ting is though that a professional might be able to tell things different about him, as well as his mom and I, because we have gone through the tests with him. But any John Doe would never see anything different about him.

And, well, as my older son says since his brother was born; "Yup, that's my little brother. I will always be keeping an eye on him!"

I hope that you do not mind my saying but I love both of my boys more than anything or anyone else in the world!

After being in my apartment for a while, things get a bit different. I start to get very small brown spots on my legs. They seem to come out of nowhere. I take some time looking at my legs but they, again, are coming out of nowhere. I try to just brush them off. No go. I try to wipe time with a wed cloth. Nothing. I put some lotion on them. Nothing. Eventually, they start an annoying feeling. The feeling continues to slight pain.

I call my doctor and he looks at them and admits me to the hospital to look at overnight. The next day there is some uneasy feeling, but not as much pain. But some. So, after another day, he releases me. Home I go. The pain has stopped and all is going OK. Well, that is, for now. About a month later, the spots start again. So does the pain, but a bit rougher now. Again I call my doctor and again he admits me and he gives me some pain killers. And, well, again, I get released again. With some stronger pain pills.

Eventually I get home and he recommends an "artificial whirlpool" for my tub. As sensitive as my legs are getting, maybe the water will release the spots. No go.

By now though I have been admitted to one hospital five times and another hospital once. The problem, is though that no one has an idea what is going on. My doctor has started me on codeine and tylenol to start and now has me taking morphine pills four to six times a day! My insurance company that is covering me because of my working when this whole thing has started has hired a nurse to be with me at home. I am now sleeping twenty hours a day and not enough energy to eat! To say nothing about the lack of strength to cook!

During my final visit, I've had a discussion with my doctor. After all of these hospital admissions, I was at my last stage. Again, I have asked the doctors and again they have said that they have no idea what is going on. I told them that I was going to take care of the problem myself. I told them that I was going to commit suicide. The docs sort of laughed. The have reminded me that I live in a wheel chair, which is across the room. I cannot walk. I am admitted into the hospital. How in the world was I going to do this?

I explained that it was rather simple. I was just going to stop eating. After four days or so, they realized that I was not playing games. They sent down the head psychologist from the hospital to talk with me. He came back with the results that, I think, shocked everyone. He said that I had no problems with my mind or my thoughts! With my being admitted six times with nothing clear, I was with "sound mind!

This last time in the hospital was my final visit. I called Paul to come over to visit me in the hospital and to please bring a notepad and a pen. Paul knows that I do not ask for visits. Especially from Danbury C to New Haven CT. Eventually he has made the trip. We discussed what my thoughts were and why and broke everything down. Honestly, he was in tears. I was not because, to me, I was thinking logically and seriously. Keeping the soft spot out.

While Paul is there, a doctor came in and we talked for a bit. Then he brought out some papers and ex-rays. He said that he finally had an idea of what was happening. Recirculating System Dysfunction, RSD. He pitched his story. Then I ask what is to be done to straighten things out. He suggested amputating the feet at the calf. When I asked if he thought that the situation would be taken care of, he replied like about any doctor would, "I'll give it a ninety percent yes".

I said OK and I asked him for something when he leaves the room. He said, 'Sure. What's that?

I replied, "a burger please! I said that I was going to commit suicide if you guys could not come up with anything. Well, this is at least something!"

So, well, down went the burger! Surgery was set for two days out. All went well and I was released back to Gaylord Rehab for more physical therapy. I was there for about a month or so and then came home again.

I had finally re-started my job again. All went well for about six months. Then, well, the other leg started with the brown marks and pain. So, again, I called my doctor. He got me into his office quickly and he re-evaluated again. He agreed that, yes, it does look similar to the other leg. By now though, he wanted to start me on pain killers. I refused them. When asked why, I replied "Look, we both know where this is going. Let's just do the amputation before we go nuts again: He agreed and the second surgery was done two or three days later. That is to say, along with my third trip to Gaylord!

My time in rehab at Gaylord went, I guess as anyone can say, went OK. Some of the staff know me by face and name. But they treat me like any new client or patient. This is actually good to me. I really hate being treated like someone special!

The way that I look at myself, I am just like anyone else. The only difference between me and you is that you have two legs and I have six wheels!

Well now, where was I? Oh yeah! As I HOPE that most people can see by reading this, I hate doing nothing. I mean, hey, when I was living in my group home in Brookfield, at Sears. It was just short of one year after my accident that I have started working. Plus, in between surgeries! Some people get shocked and approach me with, "Gary, you have been through so much!"

People say the old fashion term that God does not give you more than you can handle. I totally understand that…in a way.

You see, the way that I look at things is that life is what happens to EVERYONE. However, the important thing is what you do about it!

For example, as I explain to almost everyone that I talk with is that life is what happens with my car accident. But then, it is MY choice to do something about it all.

I could have laid in the rehab bed and said, "Whoa is me" or, as the decision that I made, I decided to FIGHT the physical problems and to show them my boys what it means to fight everything and go for it!

Hey, everyone has the right to make almost every decision of the day. Start with "Am I going to get out of bed to go to work". Most people make the right decision and get up and move. Some people might have a cold or the flue. They put that into their decision.

But, then again, there are the ones who just lay around and collect the government check. Yes, I do collect a partial check. However, I work part time at a regular job so, what I take out each month, is almost what I put in each month too. Plus, well, with what I do at work is something too.

Chapter 14

After a while of all of the surgeries and sicknesses and all, I am ready to get back out and hit the town working. I will not just hang around and watch the paint dry anymore.

Well, as everyone reading this by now knows that I am a Vet. West Haven CT has a Veterans VA Medical Center. Medical centers and hospitals are one in the same. Both can contain a variety of medical offerings, emergency treatment, primary care physicians and surgeons to name a few.

After speaking with my insurance company and others, I am getting in touch with an agency within the hospital that handles vets that have certain medical and mental problems, like me. Yes, I say mental problems just because of the Traumatic Brain Injury.

You see, my head not as tight as a normal guy. But, the best part of all, is that I can blame almost anything on TBI!

Kidding. Actually, for the most part, my head is OK. The biggest problem that I have is my memory. If I do things over and over and ove½ everything works out OK. My memory from when I was a little kid is alright too. Is just them middle part that I have problems with. I can recall a few days ago, but if someone says that I met them two or three years ago, things get fuzzy. To be honest, some things I cannot remember at all. I also have problems with numbers.

Before my accident, I use to deal with fie to fifteen dollars monthly with Xerox equipment and machines. There is no way that I can do that now. No, I do not forget what money is or how to deal with it.

Is just the numbers overall is a bit...uummm...iffy.

Eventuality I am in touch with the VA Hospital and explain my status with them. They put me in touch with an organization, The Kennedy Center. Basically, I need an organization like this to help me get associated with the VA. Is sort of like "If you are well enough to contact them myself, I should not need the assistance". Is a harsh way to look at it but hey, reality! What a concept!

So I get in touch with them and the organization, **CWT**, "Compensated Work Therapy". Their goal is "To help people get back to work" I know it sounds simple, but it is just what they do. And, if I might add, very successfully.

SO now, I am in touch with the representatives and they have a new position opening. It turns out that is position is opening as we speak. The job is with the Chaplains.

The Chaplains group has about five to seven Chaplains in the group. I say five to seven because some of the preachers are full time, like the Roman Catholic. And some are part time, like the Jewish. So when a priest is needed for whatever situation, they are able to handle it.

The Head Chaplain, is, to me, a bit scary. Please do not take this the hard way at all! He just makes me nervous because he has the right answer for the question. He is very confident in his position and, if I may say, seems to handle it well. No, he is not like a guy that people can suck up to, yet, he seems to discuss and handle and solve the situation.

He soon sits me down and we discuss my situation. I mean from home to my amputations. This way, he knows what he is dealing with.

The folks from CWT eventually come into the office and we discuss my position with them also. I am a part time employee so I do not have to worry about full time benefits. I get my pay bi-weekly along with my check and vacation scheduled and time off.

My position is clear. That is, not one of the harder things to do in like. However, it must be done accurately.

As it is explained to me, doing what I will be doing will save each Chaplain one to two hours a week in their patient visits. I have a CWT Assistant working with me. They put one there, a "normal" guy to make sure that someone else knows what I am supposed to be doing. Someone that can answer some questions and, well, I guess just to make sure that I can be close to "normal" too.

I am so happy that I am getting out of the house to work and to get things done. Having an aid come by to help me up in the morning. Then she helps me into the shower. I can do the shower myself, thank you! Then she helps me get out, helps me get dressed and makes me my morning coffee and easy breakfast. Then I take the elevator from my apartment, downstairs and take a quick run to the bus stop. I take the bus to the VA Hospital, get into my office and start my day. Just like almost everyone in town! Like a "normal" guy.

I am there, not as often as I would like, but often and long enough to get the job done. Eventually, the CWT guy goes away and all is cool. That is, for a while now. For a few years.

I have to give both of my boys a lot of credit. My oldest, like me, has no problems with working. Whatever the job. For example, he needs some money for his life, as well as his car. So, he gets a job delivering pizzas in town. Well, even though he does his job well and makes some good tips, he has decided that he will be needing or wanting some more cash. So, no, he does not go into his mothers or step-dads draws! Instead, he decides to deliver MORE pizza. He has no problem delivering for three pizza places! And, well, he does not even get a ticket for speeding or anything!

I am working now, picking up my boys every other weekend and every Tuesday after school. Then they go home after dinner, with my handicap van. Just like any divorced family. That is, for a while until I get into a discussion with my X.

As I am told, her now husband wants to leave his job up her and wants to move to Tennessee to write country music songs. I, obviously, have no concern over this, except that they are going with our boys! This does not make me a happy camper at all. When her husband and I talk, and I use the term lightly, about the boys, I ask what they have thought about my seeing them. His reply is that he plans on doing so well that he will send them back here three times a year. Again, not too good in my eyes.

About a week later, call an attorney that specializes in child custody and care. He and I sit down to see what my options are. As he basically tells me that all three of us will have to go to court and I will have to prove to the judge that I can be a more fit father to them than their mom and step dad can be.

Being that the boys have lived all their lives in their town and only been into my town, but not even the schools, plus with me living in a two-bedroom apartment, my being "disabled" and there only being one of me and tow parents at home, I decide to pay the attorney his five hundred dollars that he has earned and say Thank You, but no thanks.

The X and her husband ask me if I can keep the boys for a week or two while they take a run down to their new area to look at houses and to see about making a final determination if they are going to move away. The boys and I have no problem with this. I try to keep an upper mood of all because I do not think that it would be right fighting and running around and seeing lawyers and judges and anyone else. Besides, I know that the guys will be missing me. Hey, even though it might have been part-time, I DID help to raise them! I appear good in front of them, but inside I am between hating and fight with their step-dad. But, again, I am trying to be the big guy! No, not by running into anything, but rather to, as I have ALWAYS taught them "Do the best you can with what you've got". They know that I do not have much to me. But whatever I have in my heart and soul they can see it and feel it!

Eventually they all sell the house and all move away. This is harder for me then I thought it would be. I thought that I am a MAN! I can handle anything! OH MAN!!! AM I WRONG!!

The first Christmas that boy boys were not here, I never decorated the house, put up a tree or taped up any cards. Without them, I am nothing. Granted, I am not the guy that is sitting around in his bedroom staring at walls twiddling my thumbs. Beside, as I've said MANY times before, this thing called LIFE continues to go on.

Awhile after their move, I fly down to see them. Man how they have grown! They are both still in school and they introduce me to their favorite friends. By the looks of things, they seem to be keeping with the right buddies. Yes, I get some stories from their mom about one did this or the other did that. But, either way, neither of them are in the hospital with gunshots or knives, and neither of them are in jail. So I guess something OK came out of them with me being involved. And, I am not too crazy to say it, but I guess their step-dad was doing some things OK too.

My oldest graduate's high school. I have flown town to see this just for itself! After all, I am still their dad!

After a while, my second one graduates. You remember, the one with ADHD? Well, I have got to say that whomever took the tests with him has some serious learning to do! First off, he graduated with no problems at all! Then, he went to school to be a professional welder! There are nine different areas or types if welding. He elected to start and complete two. One right after the other!

Now, let me give you a heads up about both of these guys:

One day while my boys were over at my apartment, I spoke with the oldest about some money I had been saving for him. As I explained it, that he could use the cash either for his car or for additional school. The choice was his. He told me right away, "I need the money for my car." I told him to hold on and think about it for a day or two. This, I told him, was a one shot deal.

A couple of days later, we talked and I gave him his money for his car. He was smart and adult enough to use it for his car because he knew that he needed his car for work as well as to get around.

When my lil' guy graduated, I gave him the same option. Granted, he was living down south at the time, but he had the same options with the same amount of cash.

His reply shocked me! He explained that being that the school had him named as ADHD, his state decided to pay for him to go to school! Plus, he told me, he has two cars and they both run just fine. So, he told me to keep my own money and so whatever I wanted to! He does not want it! If I were no in a chair, I think I am going to fall over!!

Then, well, a little while after this, my oldest is seeing a girl down south. He is also having problems with his step-dad. So, he is calling me to ask if the two of them could come up here for a while. Of course I have no problem with it. They always know that my door is always open for them.

About a week or so after they are driving up to move in. He has also s shocked me telling me that I am about to be a grandfather! Of course I am shocked! Me? Grandfather? At 48?? **WOW!!**

But they are up here and all goes well except that his now-wife misses her mom and family. So, they move back down there.

Chapter 15

And now it is 2009. The boys have moved away for a while now. I feel like I am doing OK, but I guess my boss see otherwise. Again, he is a very supportive guy. As well as a great body reader and making the correct assessments. I have been down to see my guys several times. But, well, I still miss them a lot.

My boss and I sit down for a discussion. I have been doing OK with work. Eventually he asks me something that I did not expect yet should have. He inquires as to whether I have any intentions of moving away to be near them or stay up here. Although I had some quick thoughts of it, I have decided not to move. On the several times that I have flown down to see the boys I have quickly looked at the towns surrounding them. But I am not too crazy about the looking for a new place, packing, moving and unpacking and all of the running around that I will have to do long distance.

However, I have had some discussions with my insurance company with my still living in an apartment. I speak with them and explain that I am tired of an apartment and want to move into a house.

The reason, I explain, is that I want to have something to hand down to my boys.

They are a bit shocked and explain that they are not willing to buy me a house. I tell them that this is a good thing. I do NOT want them to buy me one. I explain I would like some help putting a deposit on a house and have it updated for my chair and I. After that, I would be totally responsible for the mortgage as about all other normal folks are. We all agree to it.

So now, my looking around is being done and I find a place. Nice place with a wood burning fireplace and 3 bedrooms. My first thought, though, is that I need it close enough so that I can take my chair to work. No driving! I would save so much on gas! Plus the parking at the VA is tight. So, after a while, all is said and done, I am a new owner!

The time has gone on now. It is 2017. My boss has submitted me for CLERK OF THE YEAR! There are only about five or six clerks submitted throughout the entire Hospital!

Well, no I have not been the chosen ONE, but **WOW!** Just to be brought up for the award is so fantastic!

Well maybe another time! Again, some of my favorite thoughts:

After all, this thing called LIFE happens when you are making plans.

As I have taught my boys:

If you do want to go for something more... GO FOR IT.

But, if you do not reach it, do not get upset. You still have to live with yourself and others.

Just try again!!!

-END-

www.ingramcontent.com/pod-product-compliance
Lightning Source LLC
LaVergne TN
LVHW040100080526
838202LV00045B/3718